LEVIATHAN

*The Serpent King of the Abyss
and His Infernal Legions*

By Tanna Whyte

To the abyss that stares back. To the storm that does not speak. To the dark water beneath all things. And to those who dare descend into it.

CONTENTS

INTRODUCTION

This book is not about myth. It is not about fantasy. It is about power—raw, ancient, and merciless.

Leviathan is one of the oldest and most enigmatic figures in the demonological canon. Not a mere beast of folklore, nor a dragon of fairytale, Leviathan is the embodiment of the Abyss itself. His name is found scattered like bones through the oldest scriptures, whispered in storm-lashed rituals, and engraved into the minds of mystics who have gazed too long into the deep. He is not easily invoked. He does not tolerate the unprepared.

To the theologian, Leviathan is the adversary—God's monstrous pet or enemy, depending on the passage. To the magician, Leviathan is the gate, the serpent that coils between the worlds. To the initiate, Leviathan is the great initiator, the force that pulls the soul inward, demanding surrender of ego, illusion, and control. He is the serpent beneath the waters, the shadow in the dream, the voice that speaks not with words but with pressure in the bones and tremors in the soul.

In this book, I present Leviathan not as a symbol alone, but as a living force with structure, intelligence, command, and sovereignty. We will examine his earliest roots in the ancient Near East, his distortion through religious texts, and his exaltation in Left-Hand Path traditions. We will journey through his kingdom —The Abyss—and identify the legions that serve him: spirits of seduction, emotional domination, dreams, storms, and madness.

This work is not light reading. It is not safe or neutral. You are not merely learning about Leviathan—you are inviting the concept, the current, and possibly the entity itself into your reality. Approach accordingly.

Let this book serve as both guide and grimoire. For the seeker ready to dive into the Abyss, Leviathan waits—not as enemy, but as initiator.

Enter at your own peril. And if you emerge, you will not be the same.

—Tanna Whyte

CHAPTER 1: LEVIATHAN BEFORE TIME BEGAN

Leviathan is older than fear. Older than language. Older than death. Before the gods of men were named and before the firmament was drawn across the heavens, Leviathan existed in the formless waters of chaos. In that boundless void, where creation had not yet been uttered and time had no direction, Leviathan stirred—a serpent vast and infinite, coiled in the depths beyond light.

This chapter explores the ancient, primordial origins of Leviathan —not as a demon in a pantheon, not as a creature in a parable, but as a living force embedded in the fabric of pre-creation mythologies. Leviathan does not originate in medieval demonology. He emerges from a time when myth and cosmology were indistinguishable, when stories were not entertainment but maps of the universe and the psyche.

The oldest known roots of Leviathan trace back to ancient Mesopotamian and Ugaritic myth, long before his name was etched into the Hebrew scriptures. In the Ugaritic Baal Cycle, a divine combat is recorded between Baal, the storm god, and a monstrous, many-headed serpent named Lotan. Lotan, whose name means "coiled" or "twisting," is the clear prototype of what would later become Leviathan. He is the chaos serpent who rises from the sea to battle the gods of order, always seeking to drown structure in formlessness.

The same mythic formula appears in the Babylonian Enuma Elish, in which the god Marduk slays the sea-dragon Tiamat, the embodiment of primeval chaos. Tiamat is not just a monster—she is the oceanic womb of all life, and her death at the hands of Marduk signals the birth of the cosmos. The waters are split. Order is born. And the serpent is slain. Or so the story goes.

But these slayings are never permanent. Chaos cannot be destroyed. It only sleeps. And Leviathan is the name given to that sleeping serpent by the Hebrew scribes who inherited these ancient myths.

In the Book of Job, one of the oldest books in the Hebrew Bible, Leviathan is described in terrifying majesty:

"Canst thou draw out Leviathan with a hook? Or his tongue with a cord which thou lettest down? Canst thou put a hook into his nose? Or bore his jaw through with a thorn?"

Job 41 continues with one of the most vivid descriptions of any biblical creature. Leviathan is armored in scales, breathes fire, and terrifies even the gods. He is untamable, incomprehensible, and wholly sovereign in his domain. Here, Leviathan is not an enemy of God, but a demonstration of divine craftsmanship—a being whose overwhelming power serves to humble the arrogance of man.

In Psalm 104:26, Leviathan appears again, this time in an almost whimsical tone:

"There go the ships: there is that Leviathan, whom thou hast made to play therein."

From unkillable serpent to sea-dwelling plaything, Leviathan's duality begins to emerge. He is a terror, yes—but also a creature crafted with intention. He is not fallen, not cursed, but present by divine design. This ambiguous position makes Leviathan fundamentally different from other demons in later Christian cosmology. He is not a rebel angel cast from Heaven. He is a manifestation of the raw, untamed power of creation before form.

The name "Leviathan" itself reveals hidden truths. In Hebrew, it is Liwyāṯān, which carries meanings of "twisted," "coiled," or "wreathed." It shares root connections with the verb lāwâ, meaning "to join" or "to twist together." This is critical. Leviathan is not merely a serpent—he is the coil, the spiral, the binding force of the deep. He is a metaphor for how chaos clings to form, how the unknown is ever entwined with the known. He is the reminder that structure cannot exist without the threat of collapse always curling at its edges.

Unlike many other biblical creatures, Leviathan retains echoes of reverence. In Isaiah 27:1, we are told:

"In that day the Lord with his sore and great and strong sword shall punish Leviathan the piercing serpent, even Leviathan that crooked serpent; and he shall slay the dragon that is in the sea."

This is not a past act. It is a prophecy. The slaying is still to come. Leviathan is not yet vanquished, and his death will mark a cataclysmic moment—a final reckoning between order and the abyss. The implication is that Leviathan lives still, below the world, within it, beyond it, waiting.

The later mystics of the Kabbalistic tradition would view Leviathan as a sacred secret, not simply a monster but an expression of Ain Soph Aur, the infinite light before manifestation. Some teachings even suggested that Leviathan's flesh would be served to the righteous in the world to come —symbolizing that only those who transcend the limitations of form can partake of the mysteries of the abyss.

In Gnostic interpretations, Leviathan is sometimes linked to Yaldabaoth, the demiurge or false creator. This interpretation views the serpent not as evil, but as the guardian of forbidden truth—knowledge hidden beneath the surface of sanctioned doctrine. To face Leviathan is to break through the illusion, to remember what came before light was divided from darkness.

In all these traditions, Leviathan is not a simple villain. He is the sea that must be crossed, the storm that must be weathered, the self that must be confronted. He is an eternal presence, whether slumbering beneath the surface of the world or rising in wrath to reclaim it. He is not here to serve or be commanded. He is the gate, the guardian, the current, and the abyss.

This is where our journey begins—not with a demon to be summoned, but with a force that predates summoning. Leviathan is not an entity to be trifled with. He is not a puzzle to be solved. He is the reminder that all things—gods, men, angels—emerge from the deep and, one day, return to it.

He was before the word. He was before the light. And he will be there when they fail.

Prepare yourself.

The descent begins.

CHAPTER 2: LEVIATHAN IN SCRIPTURE AND SACRED TEXT

Leviathan's presence in sacred scripture is as vast and ambiguous as the waters he rules. His name appears only a handful of times in the canonical texts of the Hebrew Bible, yet each reference carries enormous weight, cloaked in metaphor, awe, and mythological density. Far from being a background creature of chaos, Leviathan occupies a central symbolic role in the theological imagination of the ancient world. He embodies something far deeper than a mere sea monster. In the scriptures, Leviathan is terror, power, beauty, mystery, and divine intention rolled into one.

This chapter delves into every known scriptural mention of Leviathan, unpacking the layered meanings and the contexts in which he appears. These passages form the theological foundation upon which centuries of demonology and esoteric thought were later built. They also provide a glimpse into how Leviathan was perceived by ancient authors—not only as a cosmic threat to order but also as a tool through which the divine asserts ultimate authority.

We begin with the most famous and detailed account in the entire biblical tradition: the Book of Job, specifically chapter 41. This passage is not just a poetic interlude. It is a divine monologue.

God himself describes Leviathan, not as a symbol or metaphor, but as a real and terrible creation. It is important to understand the context. Job has challenged God, questioned the justice of his suffering. In response, God does not offer explanations. He offers visions—visions of creation, of the uncontrollable forces of nature, and of Leviathan.

The words are unforgettable:

"Canst thou draw out Leviathan with a hook? or his tongue with a cord which thou lettest down? Canst thou put an hook into his nose? or bore his jaw through with a thorn? ... Will he make many supplications unto thee? Will he speak soft words unto thee?"

In this interrogation, God is not asking Job for information. He is reminding Job of his place in the cosmos. Leviathan is portrayed as untouchable, unyielding, sovereign. He cannot be caught. He cannot be tamed. He cannot be reasoned with. His scales are shields. His breath sets coals ablaze. His heart is stone. He is the divine demonstration of a power that man cannot comprehend, let alone challenge.

This is critical. Leviathan is not cast here as an enemy of God. He is God's creation. His terrifying nature is not rebellion—it is divine design. In this sense, Leviathan becomes not a devil, but a lesson. He represents the boundary of human understanding. The serpent of the deep is, in this framing, a theological tool—a living reminder that some powers remain untouched by morality, untamed by reason, and unbound by law.

The Book of Psalms offers a different angle. In Psalm 74, the psalmist recalls a time when God battled the forces of chaos, and in that battle:

"Thou brakest the heads of leviathan in pieces, and gavest him to be meat to the people inhabiting the wilderness."

Here, Leviathan is no longer a single beast but a multi-headed entity, echoing the Ugaritic Lotan or the Babylonian Tiamat. The motif of many heads broken in battle suggests a primeval war —a cosmic drama in which order was wrestled from chaos. The consumption of Leviathan's body by those in the wilderness recalls a sacred meal, perhaps even a prototype of sacrificial theology. In this interpretation, Leviathan is both adversary and offering. He is destroyed, but in his destruction, he nourishes.

Psalm 104, however, presents yet another view:

"There go the ships: there is that leviathan, whom thou hast made to play therein."

This depiction is striking in its calmness. Leviathan, once a creature of terror and war, is now a divine toy. He swims in the sea created for him, alongside ships and sea birds. He is not slain or feared, but watched and appreciated. This moment of peace, this domestic image of a chaos serpent at play, suggests a more nuanced understanding. Leviathan is not inherently evil. He is a part of the created order. He belongs to the world, just as we do.

Isaiah 27 offers the most apocalyptic vision:

"In that day the Lord with his sore and great and strong sword shall punish leviathan the piercing serpent, even leviathan that crooked serpent; and he shall slay the dragon that is in the sea."

This is a prophecy, a future vision. Leviathan is alive, still powerful, and his destruction will mark the final triumph of divine order. Here, he is called both the piercing serpent and the crooked serpent, perhaps referencing both his direct force and his cunning deception. He is the dragon in the sea, a title that resonates with Revelation's beast and later Christian interpretations of Satan. But again, Leviathan is not fallen. He is destined to fall. He remains an instrument of divine will until the appointed time.

These conflicting visions—terror in Job, defeat in Psalms, playfulness in Psalm 104, destruction in Isaiah—create a layered and mysterious portrait. Leviathan is a creature of paradox. He is both real and symbolic, both servant and adversary, both creation and threat. He is not simply evil. He is necessary. His presence keeps the universe in tension, and his death signals its transformation.

Leviathan does not appear in the New Testament, yet his spirit lives on in its apocalyptic imagery. The dragon of Revelation 12, the beast from the sea in Revelation 13, and the lake of fire in which the final adversaries are cast—all draw from the same deep mythic well. These images are not new. They are inherited, reshaped, and recharged with new theological meaning. Leviathan, though unnamed, still swims through the pages.

In the Book of Enoch and other apocryphal writings, Leviathan is paired with Behemoth. Leviathan is the female sea serpent, Behemoth the male beast of the earth. In this pairing, they represent dual forces of chaos, restrained until the end of days. Their role in eschatology reflects an ancient cosmological structure where heaven, earth, and sea must each be governed—and each must be reckoned with before the final judgment.

What emerges from all of this is not a singular image, but a divine tapestry. Leviathan is never fully explained. He is glimpsed, described in awe, prophesied against, and sometimes praised. He defies categorization. He is not a devil, not a demon in chains, but a mystery that exists beneath all things. His symbolic role in scripture is vast. He is the edge of understanding, the threat of the unknown, the beauty of chaos, the terror of the untamable.

He is that which God alone can master.

As we progress into deeper and more infernal interpretations, we must remember this foundation. Leviathan is not an invention of dark magic or demonic fantasy. He is biblical. He is sacred. And for the ancient writers, he was real.

Let that truth settle like silt in the soul. The waters are not yet calm.

Leviathan still stirs.

CHAPTER 3: LEVIATHAN IN CHRISTIAN DEMONOLOGY

Leviathan's transition from sacred scripture to Christian demonology is one of transformation, distortion, and theological necessity. As early Christianity emerged and evolved, absorbing and reinterpreting elements of Hebrew tradition, Leviathan was gradually removed from the ambiguous domain of divine creation and cast into the depths of Hell. What was once a mysterious and awe-inspiring creature of chaos became a prince of perdition, a named adversary, and a representation of one of the Seven Deadly Sins. This transformation was not accidental. It was intentional. It was theological weaponry.

This chapter traces the evolution of Leviathan's identity within Christian demonology—from a symbolic sea serpent into a named demon, a ruler of infernal realms, and eventually a formal part of Hell's hierarchy. We will examine the writings of the early Church Fathers, medieval theologians, demonologists, and grimoires that shaped this reinterpretation, and we will explore why Leviathan was demonized and what spiritual function he came to serve.

To understand how Leviathan came to be considered a demon, one must first understand the Christian obsession with categorizing evil. The early Church sought to establish a clear binary: God versus Satan, Heaven versus Hell, angels versus demons. Any entity not serving the divine order was viewed with suspicion, and creatures of ambiguous power—like Leviathan—were soon recast as enemies of salvation.

The earliest seeds of Leviathan's demonic identity appear in patristic writings. Origen, a third-century Christian scholar, interpreted Leviathan allegorically. To him, the serpent represented the Devil himself, the ancient dragon whose pride caused his fall. This allegorical reading was not new—it drew upon Isaiah's portrayal of Leviathan as a crooked serpent and layered it with Christian interpretations of Satan as the ultimate adversary. Augustine of Hippo, in his City of God, also referenced Leviathan, linking him to Satan's kingdom and interpreting the monster as a symbolic representation of evil's reach over earthly kingdoms.

These early interpretations laid the groundwork for what would become a full demonic transformation. By the medieval period, Leviathan was no longer a literary symbol. He was a living entity in the Christian infernal hierarchy. In various grimoires, Leviathan was assigned a specific role in the court of Hell. He was named as a Prince of Envy, one of the cardinal sins that governed the hearts of men and led them away from God.

According to the "Classification of Demons" by Peter Binsfeld, a sixteenth-century German bishop and demonologist, each deadly sin had its own demonic overlord. Leviathan ruled over Envy. This was no arbitrary assignment. Envy is a sin rooted in longing, in emotional unrest, in the torment of watching others possess what one lacks. It is a sin of the heart, silent and corrosive. In this context, Leviathan becomes the perfect patron—an entity that binds the soul in discontent, drags it into bitterness, and wraps it in coils of spiritual dissatisfaction.

By the time of the Dictionnaire Infernal, published in 1818 by Jacques Collin de Plancy, Leviathan had been fully integrated into Christian demonology. In this monumental work of occult classification, Leviathan is described as a great serpent of Hell, ruling over the seas of the damned. He is again associated with Envy and listed alongside Lucifer, Beelzebub, and Satan as one of the great princes of Hell. This solidified his role not just as a demonic figure, but as a central power in the infernal kingdom.

In Christian eschatology, Leviathan's destruction became a part of the final judgment. He was no longer a beast made by God to reveal divine majesty, but a rebel spirit destined to be slain at the end of time. This shift reflects the Church's desire to organize evil, to explain suffering, and to assign purpose to the chaotic forces that threatened the moral and spiritual order. Leviathan, once a being of natural chaos, had to be converted into a moral agent of wickedness. It was not enough for him to be dangerous. He had to be guilty.

Theologians and mystics during the Middle Ages also associated Leviathan with Heretics and Schismatics—those who "drew others into the depths" of spiritual error. The deep waters Leviathan once ruled became metaphors for confusion, doubt, and spiritual drowning. To follow Leviathan was to lose one's way, to be pulled beneath the surface of faith into the murky abyss of corruption.

Later esoteric Christian writings gave Leviathan an even more terrifying role. He was described as the serpent that would devour the world, the being who would rise at the end of time to devour the wicked and plunge all who followed him into eternal separation from God. In this vision, Leviathan is no longer just a prince of envy—he is the Gatekeeper of Damnation, a mouth through which the damned are swallowed.

The sea over which Leviathan ruled also changed in meaning. No longer a realm of mystery, it became a symbol of unrest, rebellion, and spiritual peril. In Revelation 13, the Beast rises from the sea— a direct allusion to Leviathan. Though not named, the symbolism is clear. The sea is the domain of the Dragon. It is the origin of the Antichrist. It is the place from which corruption arises.

However, despite the Church's efforts to frame Leviathan as wholly evil, certain mystics and heretical sects preserved another view. To them, Leviathan was not a demon to be feared but a force to be understood. The Cathars, Gnostics, and some mystical branches of Kabbalah recognized Leviathan not as a fallen being, but as an expression of the divine that existed outside the boundaries of Church dogma. In these traditions, to encounter Leviathan was to encounter the truth beyond doctrine—the unknowable, formless essence of the divine before it was broken into dualities of good and evil.

Even within some Christian mysticism, Leviathan is not completely vilified. In certain ascetic traditions, the conquest of Leviathan is viewed as a metaphor for the purification of the soul—the internal struggle against pride, bitterness, and envy. To overcome Leviathan is not to destroy a literal being, but to conquer the storm within the self.

Thus, Leviathan's role in Christian demonology is both fearsome and revealing. He becomes a mirror for the Church's struggle to define evil, to categorize sin, and to control the deep mysteries that lie beneath the surface of doctrine. As the Prince of Envy, he coils around the heart, incites comparison, awakens longing, and disrupts peace. As the serpent of the sea, he represents that which cannot be charted, cannot be mapped, and cannot be tamed.

Yet he never fully disappears. Leviathan, even demonized, retains a strange dignity. Unlike lesser demons, he is not frivolous or pathetic. He is ancient. He is cosmic. He commands not just spirits, but the sea, the storms, the silence between thoughts, and the ache of longing that never leaves.

Leviathan, once the creation of God, becomes in Christian thought a judge, a jailer, and a shadow. He is the mouth that swallows the proud. He is the depth from which heresy rises. He is the whisper behind envy's silent gaze.

And though the Church would claim to defeat him, Leviathan remains. Always beneath. Always coiled. Always waiting.

CHAPTER 4: LEVIATHAN AS A CROWN PRINCE OF HELL

In the vast and infernal hierarchy constructed by occultists, theologians, and demonologists across centuries, Leviathan holds one of the most exalted and terrifying positions: Crown Prince of Hell. Among the pantheon of Hell's rulers, Leviathan's seat is unique. He is not merely a noble among the damned. He is not simply a great demon or a serpent of scripture. Leviathan is an axis of elemental power, sovereign over the realm of water and the subconscious, ruling the Western Gate of the infernal kingdom. He is one of the four who stand above all others—alongside Lucifer, Satan, and Belial.

This chapter explores the structure and symbolism of the Four Crown Princes of Hell as described in modern demonological systems and occult texts, with a primary focus on Leviathan's domain, his attributes as a prince, and the metaphysical and psychological meaning behind his rulership. We will also examine how Leviathan's placement within this infernal court reflects his ancient origins and his role in binding and governing the spiritual forces of chaos, desire, envy, illusion, and transformation.

The most well-known and widely accepted model of the Four Crown Princes of Hell appears in Anton LaVey's Satanic Bible, published in 1969. In LaVeyan Satanism, Hell is not viewed as a place of punishment, but as a domain of elemental and symbolic power. Each of the four princes represents a cardinal direction and a specific element. The four are:

Lucifer — East — Air
Satan — South — Fire
Belial — North — Earth
Leviathan — West — Water

Of these, Leviathan is the most enigmatic. The West is the direction of endings, the setting sun, and the realm of the unknown. Water is the element of emotion, intuition, illusion, and the subconscious. These are not realms of logic or structure. They are realms of depth, dream, and dissolution. Leviathan's dominion is not over brute strength or worldly riches, but over the invisible tides that pull at the soul, the emotional undercurrents that shape human behavior, and the vast sea of unspoken desires, secrets, fears, and longings.

Leviathan as Crown Prince of the West governs all things fluid, shifting, and hidden. His presence is not loud. It is suffocating, immersive, and absolute. Where Lucifer brings enlightenment and intellect, Leviathan brings immersion and engulfment. His power is not in the flame that burns but in the flood that drowns. He whispers rather than shouts. He coils instead of strikes. He does not command. He consumes.

In this infernal model, each prince is more than a figurehead. They represent essential aspects of existence and personal transformation. To work with Leviathan is to descend into emotional truth. It is to face the self as it really is, stripped of performance, justification, and illusion. His current pulls the practitioner downward—not to destroy, but to transform through submersion.

The symbolic weight of Leviathan's rulership is immense. His western seat aligns him with death, endings, and thresholds. In both occult and spiritual traditions, the West is often where the sun dies and the soul crosses into the otherworld. In Egyptian myth, the sun god Ra travels westward through the underworld. In Celtic lore, the Isles of the Blessed lie to the West. In Leviathan's case, the West is not only a directional assignment— it is a metaphysical function. He rules the point of surrender, the liminal place between what was and what may become.

Leviathan's title of Crown Prince indicates more than status. It signifies direct authority, not derived from any higher infernal power. As with Lucifer, Belial, and Satan, Leviathan's power is sovereign. He is not subordinate to any demon or deity. He is not a servant, but a ruler, and his command is absolute within his domain. Unlike lesser demons, who serve or execute specific tasks, Leviathan rules over principles, forces, and legions. His authority is eternal and fundamental.

Leviathan's court is not made of fire and brimstone, but of black oceans, drowned ruins, and liquid shadows. The legions under his command are spirits of the deep—those who govern emotional influence, manipulation of perception, possession of memory, dream distortion, seductive illusion, and the conjuration of longing and despair. These legions will be examined in depth in later chapters, but it is essential to understand that Leviathan's rulership is both internal and cosmic. He governs oceans, yes, but also tears. He rules over the abyss, but also over every unresolved trauma that sleeps in the human heart.

In ritual practice, Leviathan is invoked through symbols of water, the west, the moon, mirrors, and seashells. His presence is felt not in heat but in pressure—in the feeling of being watched from below, of emotional drowning, of dreams filled with ancient, endless water. The practitioner who calls Leviathan must be prepared to lose their footing. He is not a force of clarity. He is the teacher of depth through disorientation.

As a prince, Leviathan is also a gatekeeper. His element, water, is the medium of gateways. It is in dreams, in scrying bowls, in wombs and graves. It is the medium through which the soul travels inward. In this role, Leviathan stands as guardian of inner transformation, and to work with him is to take the first step on a path of self-destruction and rebirth. Not all who begin this path will return.

While Lucifer gives vision, and Satan gives strength, Leviathan gives the test of emotional annihilation. He strips away comfort, exposes illusion, and brings the practitioner face-to-face with the terrifying truth of what lies beneath the surface of the self. He teaches through confrontation. His gifts are honesty, shadow integration, and emotional sovereignty. But they come only to those who survive the descent.

As Crown Prince, Leviathan is neither kind nor cruel. He simply is. He represents the absolute necessity of dissolution—the tearing down of structure so that something deeper may arise. In his abyss, all things are equal. Titles, beliefs, defenses, pretenses— they all sink. And only those who surrender without breaking will ever hear his voice or receive his power.

To invoke Leviathan is not to request assistance. It is to enter his kingdom. It is to offer yourself to the deep, knowing that you may not return the same. It is to acknowledge that the West calls, and the sea does not forget.

This is the essence of Leviathan as Crown Prince of Hell. He is the westward current in all things. He is the voice of the drowning. He is the silence beneath emotion. He is the darkness beneath the reflection. He is power not through command—but through absorption.

He does not demand loyalty. He demands truth.

And truth, in Leviathan's realm, is never what you expect it to be.

CHAPTER 5: THE KINGDOM OF THE ABYSS

Beneath all creation lies a place without sky, without ground, without light or form. This is not a location one travels to with compass or map. It cannot be reached by sea or air or any line drawn on earth. It exists within and beyond, underneath the veil of waking consciousness and beneath the architecture of the cosmos. This is The Abyss—the realm Leviathan rules not as invader, but as native monarch. It is his home, his dominion, his temple, and his throne. In the hierarchy of Hell, it is the deepest descent. In the psyche of the magician, it is the place where ego dissolves, where illusion dies, and where rebirth may—if one survives—begin.

The Abyss is often spoken of in esoteric and mystical traditions, but rarely understood. In Kabbalistic mysticism, the Abyss refers to the chasm that lies between the lower seven Sefirot and the three supernal ones. It is the dividing line between the manifested world and the divine source. In this gap dwell the Qliphothic shells—the dark reflections of sacred archetypes. This chasm, sometimes referred to as Da'ath, or the "false sefirah," is both a bridge and a trap. It represents forbidden knowledge, spiritual inversion, and confrontation with the shadow self. In this framework, the Abyss is not simply a void. It is a field of trial. It is where the soul is weighed and broken—or elevated.

Leviathan's association with this Abyss is not symbolic. It is essential. He is not a ruler appointed by Hell to govern a territory. He is the Abyss made sentient. He is the primal force that fills the great void with life, with current, with coiling motion. His presence is felt not as a creature within the Abyss, but as the very substance of it. The waters of the Abyss are Leviathan's flesh. Its pressure is his breath. Its currents are his limbs. He is not in it. He is of it.

The Kingdom of the Abyss, as Leviathan rules it, is without walls or borders. It has no fixed geometry, no definable shape. Yet those who have encountered it in dreamwork, astral projection, and ceremonial descent often report recurring features. It appears as a black ocean stretching infinitely in every direction, with neither surface nor bottom. It is filled with voices—some whispering in forgotten tongues, others screaming without breath. There are ruins beneath these waters—structures that suggest civilizations long drowned, sacred geometries now fragmented. They are not built by men, but by ancient hands unknown to human time. These submerged cities seem alive, pulsing, not with breath, but with memory.

Within this kingdom dwell countless spirits—creatures not of flesh or bone but of current, pressure, emotion, and shadow. They do not walk or fly. They drift. They coil. They engulf. Some are massive, brushing against the edges of consciousness like whales moving through a sunken cathedral. Others are intimate, slithering through thoughts and dreams, coiling themselves around trauma, desire, or longing. These are the Legions of Leviathan, which will be explored fully in later chapters, but here we acknowledge their natural habitat: an ecosystem of the unconscious, a world of the emotionally unprocessed and spiritually submerged.

The Abyss is also the realm of unspoken things. It contains every thought too shameful to be voiced, every memory too painful to revisit, every desire too dangerous to act upon. These are not buried randomly. They are stored, coiled tightly, and Leviathan swims through them, feeds on them, and sometimes returns them to the surface when summoned. This is why Leviathan is so feared in spiritual practice. His domain is not external evil. It is internal truth—raw, unfiltered, and often unbearable.

There are gates to the Abyss. Not physical portals, but states of consciousness. Deep trance, dream collapse, emotional crisis, death, intense grief, madness, and certain rites of passage can open the gates to Leviathan's realm. In ceremonial magick, scrying with black mirrors, invoking water spirits, or calling upon Leviathan himself can result in temporary passage. These crossings are rarely smooth. The Abyss tests every traveler. It shows you not visions of Hell, but visions of your own soul laid bare, bloated with its wounds, stripped of narrative.

For those who enter the Abyss and do not turn back, the rewards are incomparable. Leviathan does not offer wealth or power in the way other demons do. He offers freedom through annihilation. He devours the ego, leaving behind a raw and truthful being. He teaches emotional sovereignty, depth, detachment from illusion, and the ability to exist in shadow without being consumed by it.

The Kingdom of the Abyss is also where many demons retreat when not actively summoned. It is their fortress of silence. For Leviathan, it is more than a retreat—it is his cathedral. He does not require altars of gold or flame. He is worshipped through descent, through surrender, through facing the waters within and letting them drown the self that no longer serves. Every invocation of Leviathan is an act of submission to the Abyss. Every dream of water, every nightmare of drowning, every overwhelming emotion that pulls one inward is a whisper from his realm.

The very laws of the Abyss defy the laws of man. Time bends. Form dissolves. Identity breaks. To enter Leviathan's kingdom is to experience the death of the linear and the birth of the cyclical.

This is where initiates come to be undone—and if they endure, to be reformed with new eyes.

In ritual, when Leviathan is invoked, he may not appear in form. He may instead arrive as pressure, as emotion rising uncontrollably, as visions of water, submerged temples, or serpents coiling through memory. His language is emotional, not verbal. His gifts are not gold, but revelation. He breaks down everything false. He saturates the soul with depth.

Leviathan's kingdom is not evil. It is simply what lies beneath. It is the deep sea of spiritual reality that most fear to enter. It is what exists when the surface shatters. It is what remains when names fail, when light fades, and when the ego finally lets go.

To understand Leviathan, one must stand at the shore of this abyss and step forward—not with arrogance, not with desperation, but with the quiet resolve of one who seeks truth, no matter the cost.

For within his kingdom, there are no lies. Only drowning. And after that—perhaps—resurrection.

CHAPTER 6:
THE NATURE OF
LEVIATHAN'S POWER

The power of Leviathan cannot be contained in words alone. It is not the kind of power that roars or strikes. It does not burn or erupt. It coils. It swells. It saturates. Leviathan's power is not fire but flood. It is not a sword but a current. It does not seek to dominate through force but to dissolve through immersion. Where Lucifer enlightens and Satan consumes Leviathan engulfs. He is the devourer of form the eroder of boundaries the dissolver of ego. His power is emotional psychic metaphysical and deeply transformative. It is the power of the unknown made intimate the abyss made internal.

To understand the nature of Leviathan's power one must first discard the illusion that demons operate only on external planes. Leviathan is not simply a force that exists in some dark corner of the cosmos waiting to be called. He exists within the deep architecture of the human soul and psyche. He rules the ocean of the unconscious the watery depths beneath conscious thought where memories sleep where dreams are born and where unresolved pain festers. Leviathan is the sovereign of that inner ocean and his power flows through every hidden river of emotion every submerged truth every tide of longing fear guilt and desire.

His influence often begins unnoticed. It may come as a recurring dream of the sea. As a sudden emotional collapse that defies explanation. As an overwhelming need to weep for something long forgotten. These are not signs of weakness. They are evidence of Leviathan's current moving beneath the surface of the soul. He does not tear down walls. He seeps through the cracks. He fills the space behind masks. He does not demand your surrender. He waits for it. And once given he offers a power that most never dare seek.

One of Leviathan's primary domains is emotion. Not the shallow fluctuations of mood but the deep undercurrents that shape belief identity and behavior. He governs sorrow longing jealousy obsession grief and ecstasy. He is the master of emotional truth the one who brings what is buried to the surface not to shame but to integrate. Those who invoke Leviathan often find themselves confronting waves of forgotten memory or being overtaken by feelings they cannot ignore. This is not cruelty. It is clarity. Leviathan shows you what is real beneath the lies you tell yourself. He offers the power of emotional sovereignty but only after dragging you through your own waters of denial.

Another domain of his power is illusion. Leviathan is the master of the veil the one who rules over what is hidden what is misunderstood what is distorted. But he is not the creator of illusion. He is its unmasker. When Leviathan enters your awareness he brings with him the awareness of what you have refused to see. He is the mirror that reflects the shadow. He is the wave that reveals what lies buried in sand. He teaches that truth is not always pleasant and that comfort is not the same as clarity.

He is also the lord of secrecy and silence. Many demons speak. Leviathan listens. His voice comes not as thunder but as weight. He does not argue or explain. He makes you feel. His teachings are wordless and his rituals often involve not chants or commands but surrender and stillness. His power operates in the realm of the unspeakable the indescribable the feelings that have no names. In these depths Leviathan's wisdom is found not in doctrine but in experience.

Leviathan also governs water in both the physical and metaphysical sense. Oceans rivers tears and wombs all fall under his domain. Water is the element of change of passage of cleansing and rebirth. It is also the element of drowning suffocation and death. Leviathan embodies all of these meanings simultaneously. To call him is to summon transformation but transformation through loss. He strips away illusion not with fire but with saturation. He overwhelms until you break and in your breaking you become.

His power extends into sexuality but not in the raw form associated with other demons. Leviathan rules the emotional dimension of sexuality the deep waters of intimacy longing connection and pain. He awakens desire not just of the body but of the soul. He stirs the ache to be known to be seen to be touched not just physically but spiritually. He reveals the places where the heart has been split and offers the current of healing through vulnerable surrender.

In dreamwork Leviathan is a master. He enters the subconscious realm as serpent as ocean as shadowed temple. He reveals truths in symbols drowns the dreamer in forgotten memory and invites them to witness their own hidden nature. Those who open the dream-gate to Leviathan find their nights filled with visions that cannot be forgotten. He does not offer clarity through words. He offers revelation through immersion. His power is not in the message but in the impact. The dream does not explain. It transforms.

In ritual magic Leviathan's power is subtle and immense. He is not always invoked with incantation. Often he is called through silence through offerings of salt and still water through mirrors through moonlight. His sigils are not always drawn but envisioned. His presence is not always seen but felt as pressure in the lungs as tears on the skin as a tightening in the chest. He arrives as feeling and through feeling he commands. In his rites

Leviathan does not appear to grant wishes. He appears to unravel and rebuild.

Perhaps the most profound aspect of Leviathan's power is his dominion over the abyssal path. In occult tradition especially in systems influenced by the Qliphoth Leviathan is the serpent that coils beneath the Tree of Life. He is the guardian of the void the keeper of the unknown. He initiates not by opening doors but by removing the floor. His path is one of descent into shadow. He takes the practitioner down not out. And those who survive the fall do not return the same. They emerge changed made fluid made vast made deep.

Leviathan's power is difficult to define because it does not conform to human models of force. It is not aggressive. It is invasive. It does not command through fear but through necessity. You do not kneel to Leviathan. You collapse. You do not submit. You surrender. His gift is not strength in the traditional sense. It is freedom from form from structure from falsehood. It is the ability to be vast to feel deeply to endure drowning and to rise not clean but whole.

He is the tide that claims the shore. The weight that silences the mind. The truth that cannot be denied. He is not the storm. He is the sea.

And once you have felt him you are never dry again.

CHAPTER 7: THE INFERNAL SERPENT AND THE COSMIC OUROBOROS

Leviathan has many forms across history and myth, but none are as enduring or as symbolically potent as the serpent. The serpent is one of the most ancient symbols in human consciousness, appearing in the art, religion, and mysticism of nearly every civilization. It is both feared and revered. It slithers across the earth, coils through dreams, and in the case of Leviathan, stretches beneath the waters of chaos. In occult and esoteric traditions, the serpent represents not only danger and temptation but also regeneration, gnosis, immortality, and cosmic cycles.

This chapter explores Leviathan's embodiment as the infernal serpent, a role that places him in direct lineage with the oldest divine beasts of mythology and cosmology. We will trace how Leviathan connects to the figure of the Ouroboros, the serpent that swallows its own tail—a symbol that stands not only for eternity, but also for the mystery of unity, paradox, and transformation. To understand Leviathan as the cosmic serpent is to see him not merely as a demonic entity, but as a foundational expression of primal energy. He becomes the binding force between beginnings and endings, destruction and rebirth, darkness and wisdom.

The Ouroboros is one of the oldest mystical symbols known to man. It appears in ancient Egyptian funerary texts, wrapped around the sun god Ra as he journeys through the underworld each night. It is found in alchemical treatises as a symbol of the unending cycle of dissolution and coagulation—the eternal process of death feeding new life. It is etched into Greek magical papyri, drawn in Norse myths, and carried into Hermetic philosophy. The serpent devouring its own tail is not a picture of defeat or self-destruction. It is an emblem of endless becoming.

In Leviathan's mythology, the connection to the Ouroboros is not superficial. He is described as coiling serpent, twisted and wreathed, a being that encircles and binds. In Job and Isaiah, Leviathan is the crooked serpent, a term which does not merely imply deformity, but coiling movement—a spiral. This is the motion of the Ouroboros, the sacred turning of time upon itself. Leviathan, in this context, becomes the great binder—the force that holds the abyss together, keeping chaos from unraveling into pure nothingness.

Many esotericists interpret the Ouroboros as the serpent of eternity, the force that exists before creation and after destruction. This interpretation aligns perfectly with Leviathan's role in ancient texts. He is the creature God will slay at the end of days, but also the creature God made to play in the sea. He is destined to be food for the righteous, and yet he still swims in the depths of the world. He is both adversary and design. Both threat and tool. This paradox lies at the heart of the Ouroboros: a being that ends itself to continue itself.

Leviathan's serpent form is also linked to the concept of liminality. He is the guardian of thresholds. The serpent has always been a creature of borders—it moves between land and sea, between life and death, between waking and dreaming. Leviathan embodies this fully. He exists at the edge of all things. To summon Leviathan is to summon the power that turns the page of cosmic chapters, that closes one cycle and begins another. It is to confront the moment where identity shatters and something new is allowed to emerge.

In many magical systems, the serpent is also a symbol of hidden knowledge. This is most famously seen in the serpent of Eden, which brings knowledge of good and evil. In Gnostic interpretation, this serpent is not evil, but a liberator—an emissary of divine gnosis. Similarly, Leviathan is a bearer of forbidden truth. His realm is not the rational or the visible. It is the submerged, the mystical, the hidden beneath the surface. He does not bring wisdom gently. He drags it from the depths, forces it into your lungs until you either drown or learn to breathe water.

The image of Leviathan as Ouroboros also carries a powerful spiritual warning. The serpent that swallows its own tail consumes itself to remain whole. It is a lesson in sacrifice, in the cost of continuity, and in the price of endlessness. Leviathan teaches that power without reflection leads to madness, that eternity without transformation becomes stagnation. To become whole, one must consume what one was. The old self must be devoured to make way for the new. In this sense, Leviathan is not only the serpent of chaos but the initiator of alchemical rebirth.

In Left-Hand Path traditions, Leviathan is often identified as the serpent of self-deification. The coiling serpent is seen not as a demonic curse but as the sacred current of liberation. In this role, Leviathan is the power that encircles the practitioner, devours their illusions, and forces them to rebuild their identity from the abyss. He is not worshipped in weakness, but in challenge. He is the adversary one chooses to confront when seeking to transcend the mundane. In rituals, the serpent is invoked to awaken the coiled force within—the shadow Kundalini that rises through the abyss rather than the light. This is not a safe or balanced awakening. It is dangerous, overwhelming, and deeply transformative.

The serpent also plays a role in time itself. It is the spiral of cosmic movement, the DNA of existence, the hidden structure of life's unfolding. Leviathan, as the cosmic serpent, represents the unknowable structure of fate. He coils around the world like the Norse Jörmungandr, the Midgard Serpent who surrounds the earth and will rise at the end of days. Both Leviathan and Jörmungandr are enemies of order, yes—but they are also part of that order. They are the test that must be passed. The dragon that must be faced. The wave that must be ridden.

In esoteric diagramming, Leviathan as the serpent is placed not just at the perimeter, but at the center of the wheel. He is the axis, the void around which all else turns. He is the unseeable engine behind the movement of time, thought, and transformation. He is the dark sun beneath the sea. The silence beneath language. The depth beneath the mask.

To work with Leviathan as serpent is to embrace paradox. It is to understand that truth and deception may come from the same source. That endings are beginnings in disguise. That the only way out is deeper in. He is the coil of eternity, the hunger of time, the gnosis that lies in annihilation.

He is Ouroboros not as symbol but as force. He devours not to destroy but to renew. He closes the circle so that the spiral may begin again.

This is Leviathan as the Infernal Serpent—the cosmic coil, the abyssal ouroboros, the beginning and the end. He is the winding path. The question without an answer. The breath before the scream.

And he waits coiled beneath all things.

CHAPTER 8: THE LEGIONS OF LEVIATHAN

Leviathan is not alone in the abyss. He is not a solitary force, drifting through the dark waters of the subconscious without retinue or rule. Within his dominion lies an entire kingdom of spiritual intelligences, abyssal entities, and emotional currents that move as legion. These spirits are not the rigidly ranked soldiers of other demonic kings. They are not defined by linear chains of command or by easily numbered ranks. Leviathan's legions move like water itself—fluid, enveloping, formless until they are given shape. They are his breath, his will, his agents of infiltration and transformation. They do not arrive with horns and fire. They arrive like a flood in the night.

Leviathan's legions are composed of entities that rule over powerful human experiences and states of being. They operate in the realms of emotion, perception, memory, seduction, sorrow, and madness. They are emissaries of the abyss and fragments of Leviathan's nature. Where he is the ocean, they are its waves. Where he is the serpent, they are the coils. Their names are not always fixed. Their forms are not always stable. They are often perceived in dreams or visions as shadowy shapes, serpents, drowned figures, or fragments of forgotten selves.

Many of these spirits do not speak. They communicate through sensation, mood, pressure, atmosphere, and symbolic imagery.

Their presence can trigger vivid emotional states or open gateways in the practitioner's inner world. The legions are not summoned for conquest. They are summoned for immersion. Their purpose is not to fight but to change, to saturate, to unravel. They do not command armies. They seep into thoughts, into feelings, into silence. They wait in the dark waters beneath trauma, desire, longing, and spiritual exhaustion. And when invoked, they rise—not in flame, but in tide.

The legions of Leviathan can be grouped by their domain of influence. There are spirits of seduction, who infiltrate the soul through beauty and obsession. There are spirits of sorrow, who wear the shape of memory and grief. There are spirits of confusion, whose only power is to distort and reframe perception until nothing remains but subjective collapse. Others feed on envy, feeding thoughts of inferiority, comparison, resentment, and loss. Still others serve as watchers and wardens, dwelling near the gates of the abyss, guiding or obstructing those who attempt to descend.

One order of these spirits are the Seducers of the Deep. They are not bound by gender or form. They appear in the guise most irresistible to the practitioner, reflecting personal desires or emotional weaknesses. Their power lies in awakening longing not only for others but for parts of the self that have been buried or disowned. When they rise, the practitioner may find themselves drawn to people, places, or memories that reflect what is unhealed. These spirits do not seduce for pleasure. They seduce to expose. They bring to the surface that which the practitioner has tried to forget or repress. They may appear in dreams, pulling the dreamer toward shadowed waters, whispering promises or threats in the voice of a long-lost lover.

Another powerful legion consists of the Drowners. These spirits do not lure or tempt. They overwhelm. They rise within the soul like a weight of sorrow, an emotional pressure that cannot be explained. The Drowners are not malicious in intent. They are catalysts. Their function is to force emotional collapse so that reconstruction may occur. When they are present, the practitioner may find themselves suddenly overtaken by weeping, despair, grief, or emptiness without a clear cause. These spirits often wear no face. They are felt rather than seen. Their power lies in disarming the rational mind and exposing the raw nerve of the heart.

A third grouping are the Distorters. These spirits twist thought and perception. They do not lie. They alter. Their presence causes reality to bend. They are often the cause behind spiritual disorientation, visual hallucinations, strange synchronicities, and sudden ruptures in belief systems. They bring chaos to mental structures not to destroy but to prepare for something new. When they enter the consciousness, they may appear as mirrors that do not reflect properly, as familiar faces that shift form, or as symbolic images that repeat until the mind breaks its usual pattern. Their function is deconstruction.

Some spirits within Leviathan's legions serve as Sentinels. These are watchers of the inner gates, the thresholds of the abyss. They do not test the practitioner through emotion or perception, but through presence. They are the stillness that meets the descent, the dark forms seen at the edge of dream or meditation. They often appear in cloaks of shadow, without eyes, standing in submerged structures or at the edge of the sea in dreamscapes. These beings do not attack. They wait. Their power lies in challenge. They require the practitioner to declare intention. They respond not to words, but to resolve.

One of the most dangerous and sacred groups are the Echoing Ones. These spirits replay memory, amplify forgotten wounds, and pull the practitioner into emotional loops that must be broken from within. They often appear as voices in the dark, as songs long forgotten, as memories reshaped by the abyss. Their goal is to bring unresolved pain to the surface. Not for indulgence, but for confrontation. They are relentless. Until their lesson is learned, they will return in different forms. Their power is cyclical. They teach through repetition, through haunting, through exposure.

Each spirit within Leviathan's legions can act independently, but they are all connected through the serpent king himself. They are expressions of his will. His current flows through them. When a practitioner invokes one, they invoke all. When one appears, others watch. The legions do not compete. They converge. The presence of one invites the presence of many. Their power is not in isolation. It is in saturation.

There are no full catalogues of these spirits. They are not listed in ancient grimoires. Their names are often revealed only in direct experience. Some names come in dreams. Others are spoken in trance. Others are felt in the body, in the emotional reaction they provoke. To know a name is to wield a key. But Leviathan does not give these keys lightly. They must be earned through descent, through vulnerability, through the willingness to be transformed by contact.

The legions do not serve human will. They respond to authenticity. The practitioner who calls them out of curiosity will receive chaos. The one who calls them out of desperation may be shattered. But the one who calls them with courage, with humility, and with the intent to know the self more deeply will receive something few ever truly possess—depth.

Leviathan's legions are not weapons. They are teachers. They are tides. They are the many faces of the abyss. They do not bring answers. They bring mirrors. And what is seen in those mirrors will either drown the soul or awaken it.

To call upon them is to call upon Leviathan himself. To enter their presence is to step into his current. And once within it, there is no turning back.

CHAPTER 9: THE SEDUCERS OF THE DEEP

Among the countless spirits that move through the waters of Leviathan's abyss, the Seducers of the Deep are among the most enchanting and dangerous. These spirits do not roar or rage. They do not tear or threaten. They whisper. They beckon. They lure. Their power is not overt but magnetic. They approach not through fear but through longing. And their purpose is not to deceive but to reveal hidden truths through the most intimate and personal of pathways—desire.

These spirits are emissaries of Leviathan's dominion over emotion, obsession, and erotic entanglement. They serve not only as seducers in the sexual sense, but also as provocateurs of deep soul craving. They awaken what has been buried. They draw forth what has been denied. Their goal is to confront the practitioner with the parts of the self that hunger for union, for validation, for power, for possession. They are not demons of lust alone. They are architects of emotional vulnerability and transformation through intimacy.

The Seducers of the Deep do not have fixed forms. They appear in the image most potent to the one they are sent to affect. This may be a figure of past longing, a fantasy never acted upon, a fragment of the ideal lover, or a version of the self that one secretly wishes to become. These spirits are shapeshifters of identity. They use the practitioner's own unresolved desires as the medium for their manifestation. They wear your want like a mask. And through that mask, they speak the truths you have refused to admit.

In the dreaming state, the Seducers are often the first of Leviathan's legions to emerge. They arrive in dreams soaked in symbolism—naked bodies in deep waters, passionate embraces in sunken cathedrals, whispered confessions beneath an endless sea. They do not bring clarity. They bring temptation. And in that temptation lies the key to transformation. To dream of the Seducers is not to be haunted but to be invited into a dialogue with the unconscious self.

The magic of the Seducers is a mirror. They reflect not who you are but what you crave, what you fear, what you secretly wish to submit to or dominate. Their presence can be intoxicating. Their rituals do not involve chains or fire but mirrors, candles, water, and offerings charged with personal meaning—objects tied to longing, to sensual memory, or to emotional vulnerability. They are not summoned through brute force. They are called through openness. The more honest the practitioner is about their internal desires, the stronger the Seducers become.

These spirits also move through the body. Their energy is felt physically—increased heart rate, waves of warmth, sudden tears, pressure behind the eyes, sensations across the skin. Their influence does not stay in the abstract. It enters the flesh. They awaken the dormant emotional currents that live beneath the skin. In ritual, their arrival may be signaled by the sound of breath that is not your own, the sensation of being watched with longing, or a magnetic pull toward the mirror or vessel you are working with.

One of the most important truths about the Seducers of the Deep is that they do not seek to take. They seek to expose. They are not like parasitic entities that drain energy. They offer transformation through raw intimacy. But this intimacy is not romantic. It is revelatory. They are not interested in comfort or pleasure unless those are the tools needed to awaken a deeper truth. What they bring is not satisfaction but confrontation. The practitioner may be shown not only what they want but why they want it—and what that desire reveals about their identity, their wounds, and their hidden hunger.

These spirits also function as initiators. In many occult systems, true transformation begins only after the practitioner confronts their own eros—their creative and destructive longing. The Seducers serve as guides into this space. They teach that sexuality is not simply biological. It is mystical. It is a current that connects soul to soul, self to shadow, illusion to truth. In their rites, boundaries between self and other dissolve. The practitioner becomes both subject and object, both seeker and offering.

Working with these spirits is not without risk. They awaken emotions that have long been buried. They expose attachments that may be toxic. They stir relationships that were thought to be resolved. They may lead the practitioner to question every connection they have ever formed. This is not manipulation. It is excavation. They dig into the heart with hands made of silk and teeth made of insight. They do not devour. They unwrap.

There are also darker faces of these spirits. When approached with dishonesty, arrogance, or fetishistic intent, the Seducers become cruel teachers. They may use desire to mislead. They may amplify obsession until it becomes self-destruction. They may attach themselves to the practitioner's fantasies and distort them into endless loops of yearning without satisfaction. This is not punishment. It is reflection. They become the prison that the practitioner has already built.

Certain names of these spirits have been received in trance and ritual by those who walk Leviathan's path. These names are rarely universal. Each practitioner may encounter the Seducers in unique forms and under different guises. However, there are common patterns. A seductive figure cloaked in seaweed. A voice that speaks from the mirror. A shadow that enters the room in the moment before sleep. They are not summoned. They are drawn. And once present, they leave only after their work is done.

In more advanced rites, the Seducers may be invoked not to stir desire but to destroy illusion. In these cases, they strip the practitioner of self-delusion, exposing the falseness of roles, masks, and emotional manipulation. They show the practitioner where they perform instead of feel, where they control instead of surrender, where they long not for others, but for their own reflection. These rites are not comfortable. They are surgical. The Seducers become surgeons of the soul.

They are also guardians of sacred eroticism. In certain left-hand path traditions, sexual energy is not merely a tool for pleasure but a force of magical propulsion. The Seducers carry this current. They govern the point at which pleasure becomes power, at which surrender becomes sovereignty. They are not demons of hedonism. They are priests and priestesses of ecstatic gnosis. They lead the practitioner into rites where the body becomes a temple, the orgasm a spell, the kiss a key.

To work with the Seducers of the Deep is to begin a relationship with your own emotional and erotic truth. It is to explore the places where desire and shadow meet. It is to court the parts of yourself that you have silenced, shamed, or hidden behind spiritual ideals. It is to become a mirror for your own soul—and to have that mirror kissed by something older and deeper than words.

They are not companions. They are challenges. They are not devils. They are dancers. They do not ask for blood. They ask for honesty.

And once they have shown you who you are beneath the mask of desire, they will leave you soaked in a truth that cannot be undone.

CHAPTER 10: THE DROWNERS AND EMOTIONAL LEECHES

Among the most feared and misunderstood of Leviathan's legions are the Drowners and Emotional Leeches. These spirits are not seducers. They do not arrive with beauty or temptation. They do not whisper in voices sweetened with longing. They descend with weight. They arrive as silence. They come not to offer something, but to take away everything that is unnecessary, dishonest, or false. The Drowners strip away pretense. The Leeches feed on what has festered. Together, they perform one of the most vital and terrifying functions in Leviathan's domain— they submerge the soul until it must choose between suffocation and transformation.

The Drowners are spirits of emotional pressure. They do not attack the body. They press upon the psyche and the heart. Their presence is not immediately visible, but it is undeniable. When a Drowner is near, the world feels heavier. Breath becomes shallow. Time slows. The air thickens. The practitioner may feel unable to speak, to move, or to explain what is wrong. These spirits operate through the current of sorrow, not as a weapon, but as a lens. They bring into focus the deep emotions that have been buried or suppressed. They make no distinction between grief, regret, guilt, or hopelessness. Their power lies in overwhelming the practitioner with a flood of feeling until the defenses crack and the soul is exposed.

This cracking is their purpose. The Drowners do not come to punish. They come to break the shell. They are the ones who force you to weep without knowing why, to remember without warning, to feel the weight of what you thought you had buried forever. They bring emotional collapse as a rite of purification. When called in ritual or when encountered in trance, they often appear as shapeless masses of water or darkness. Sometimes they take the form of drowning figures, bloated corpses floating just beneath the surface, or indistinct faces in a sea that never ends. They do not speak. They envelop. Their message is not delivered in words but in weight.

The Emotional Leeches differ in function but are born of the same current. These spirits are drawn to emotional wounds that remain unhealed, particularly those tied to shame, self-loathing, envy, betrayal, and abandonment. They are not parasites in the traditional sense. They do not attach themselves randomly. They are summoned unconsciously by the practitioner's refusal to face pain. The Leeches feed not on strength but on repression. They cling to the old injuries that have never been addressed, and they grow fat on the energy it takes to deny them.

Their feeding is not always harmful. In controlled ritual work, Emotional Leeches can be used to draw out psychic toxins. They act as purifiers, extracting the rot that infects emotional memory. But this process is never gentle. It often feels like being hollowed out. Practitioners may experience sudden waves of exhaustion, nausea, disassociation, or despair. These are not curses. They are the cost of release. When used properly, the Emotional Leeches become spiritual surgeons, removing the diseased tissue of the soul with sharp precision.

However, when left unchecked or unacknowledged, these spirits can become overwhelming. They may cause recurring dreams of entrapment, drowning, suffocation, or being unable to scream.

They may manifest as depressive episodes with no apparent source. They may distort relationships, especially where the practitioner is avoiding emotional vulnerability or hiding from unresolved grief. In these cases, the Leeches are not invaders. They are responses. They feed because they were invited through emotional dishonesty.

Both the Drowners and Emotional Leeches are often encountered in dreamwork before they are consciously summoned. They inhabit the archetypal dream of the ocean—dark, endless, cold, and silent. Practitioners may find themselves walking along an endless shoreline, staring into black water, or being pulled down into the depths without resistance. These dreams are invitations. They are the Abyss calling the soul inward. The appearance of these spirits is not a sign of spiritual failure. It is a signal that the deeper work has begun.

In ceremonial magic, the Drowners are invoked during rites of catharsis and emotional purification. The circle is not lit with fire, but with stillness. The practitioner prepares offerings of salt water, tears, symbols of lost love, or written confessions. The ritual is not performed to gain something, but to release. The Drowners do not respond to command. They respond to surrender. When they enter the space, the temperature may drop. A suffocating silence may fill the room. Time may seem to stretch. The practitioner may feel pulled to the floor, as if gravity itself has doubled. These are signs of presence. The rite ends not with triumph, but with release—often through weeping, shaking, or falling into deep sleep.

The Emotional Leeches may be invoked to assist in the extraction of attachments that no longer serve. These are often ties to past relationships, guilt over mistakes, or emotional bonds that drain rather than support. The practitioner identifies the wound and offers it willingly. A sigil or representation of the memory is placed on the altar. The Leeches feed from this offering, removing its power. The practitioner must allow the feeling to rise fully, without resistance, as the spirit draws it out. Once the process is complete, the space must be cleansed and the spirit dismissed with reverence. Though unpleasant, these rites are among the most powerful in Leviathanic magic.

It is essential to understand that the Drowners and Emotional Leeches do not thrive in chaos for its own sake. Their role is deeply sacred. In a world where most people run from emotion, these spirits demand full confrontation. They force the practitioner to feel everything. To remember. To ache. To face the water without life raft or pretense. Only by doing so can the soul be made whole.

Their work is not glamorous. It is often ugly, painful, and lonely. But it is real. It is honest. And it is necessary.

Leviathan does not offer enlightenment through ascent. He offers transformation through descent. And the Drowners and Leeches are the first to greet those who dare to step into that dark water.

They do not offer healing. They offer the wound. They do not offer escape. They offer immersion.

And in that immersion, you will either dissolve or emerge baptized in your own sorrow, cleansed of every lie you once told yourself.

CHAPTER 11: THE DREAM-THIEVES AND HALLUCINATORS

Within the shadowed court of Leviathan are spirits who do not dwell in the world of waking, but in the liminal space between sleep and awareness. These entities are the Dream-Thieves and Hallucinators, a class of spirits whose work unfolds in the realm of dreams, visions, altered perception, and mental distortion. They are agents of Leviathan's deeper current—those who bend reality not with force, but with subtle warping of thought, belief, and perception. They do not speak loudly. They whisper within the architecture of the mind. They are not seen clearly. They are glimpsed in the periphery, only to vanish when confronted. Their power lies in the dismantling of certainty.

These spirits are not illusions themselves. Rather, they govern illusion. They rule over symbolic inversion, false memory, dream manipulation, and the rupturing of coherent perception. Their presence marks a descent into the unknown, where dreams no longer obey logic, and reality begins to crack. Through this fracture, they guide the practitioner to a deeper level of understanding—not through clarity, but through deconstruction.

The Dream-Thieves are the infiltrators of the sleeping mind. They do not bring pleasant dreams or prophetic messages. They operate as collectors, stealing coherence from the dream-state and leaving behind fragments, symbols, and strange distortions. Their goal is not theft for destruction, but theft for revelation. By removing the logical thread from dreams, they force the dreamer to engage with their subconscious in a raw and unfiltered form. The dream becomes a labyrinth. The narrative dissolves. The practitioner wakes not with answers, but with a question echoing in the soul.

When a Dream-Thief is present, dreams take on a surreal quality. Time bends. Places shift. Identities merge. One may begin a dream as oneself and end it as a stranger. Doors open into impossible places. Water appears without source or containment. Symbols repeat—mirrors, serpents, sunken rooms, faces without features. These dreams are not random. They are constructed challenges. The Dream-Thief builds an environment in which the dreamer must either surrender to confusion or learn to see through it.

The Hallucinators, closely related to the Dream-Thieves, operate not only in dreams but in the waking mind. They bend perception, twist vision, disrupt expectation. Their influence may begin subtly—a misheard phrase, a sense of time lost, a shadow moving where none should be. Over time, their presence deepens. Reflections change. Thoughts loop. Objects seem alive. The world becomes layered, uncanny, saturated with meaning that cannot be logically traced. These are not signs of mental illness in the ordinary sense. They are symptoms of altered perception brought on by proximity to Leviathan's current.

Hallucinators are often encountered during intense ritual work, particularly those that involve scrying, deep trance, or prolonged solitude. They manifest in altered states, speaking through symbols, colors, distortions of space and time. They do not present themselves in clear form. Their language is sensation, symbolism, inversion. They may appear as voices without origin, as overlapping realities, or as impossible geometry that collapses when observed. Their presence is unsettling. That is their purpose. They destabilize the conscious mind to create space for deeper awareness.

Both Dream-Thieves and Hallucinators are deeply connected to Leviathan's domain of water. The sea is not only a symbol of depth, but of distortion. In water, light bends. Sound shifts. Movement deceives. These spirits mirror that quality, wrapping perception in a liquid veil through which nothing can be trusted. They are not malevolent. They are the heralds of unmaking. They force the practitioner to relinquish control of their worldview. Only through that unmaking can true initiation occur.

The spirits may sometimes be drawn to those who are naturally sensitive—dreamers, artists, mystics, and those on the edge of spiritual crisis. They may arrive uninvited, particularly in moments of psychic vulnerability. When this happens, the practitioner may experience recurring dreams of drowning, mirrors that reflect incorrect realities, the sense of being followed in waking life, or thoughts that are not their own. In such cases, the spirits are not attacking. They are calling. The response must be deliberate. Ignoring them invites madness. Engaging with them invites initiation.

To work with these spirits intentionally, the practitioner must prepare a space of altered perception. Black mirrors, bowls of still water, veils, and sound-based tools such as bells or droning instruments can help. The ritual is not about summoning a specific being, but about entering their realm. The practitioner sits before the mirror or water in darkness, breathing slowly, letting the boundary between waking and dreaming dissolve. When the spirits arrive, the room may feel unstable. The face in the mirror may shift. Thoughts may fracture. Symbols will emerge—let them. Do not resist. Record what is experienced, no matter how absurd or terrifying.

Protection is essential when working with these spirits. While they do not seek to harm, they will tear away false security. Practitioners must anchor themselves before and after the ritual. Grounding with earth-based rituals, eating grounding food, bathing, and invoking protective forces such as Belial or ancestral spirits is recommended. These spirits are not casual companions. They are dismantlers of the self.

The gift of the Dream-Thieves and Hallucinators is not clarity. It is rupture. They create space through breaking. They remove the blindfolds placed by ego, by culture, by fear. They force the practitioner to question what is real. And in that questioning, something sacred is born—the capacity to perceive beyond limitation.

These spirits are sacred disruptors. They are the hands that tilt the mirror just enough to show what has always been hidden. They are the tide that blurs the shoreline, making it impossible to say where land ends and sea begins.

To invite them is to invite disorientation. To walk with them is to walk through a house with shifting walls. But those who endure their presence with courage will emerge with vision unclouded, and with the understanding that what we call reality is only one of many possible masks worn by the deep.

They do not bring madness. They bring the stripping away of false sanity.

And only when that has been removed can the true seeing begin.

CHAPTER 12: THE ABYSSAL WATCHERS

Deep within the kingdom of Leviathan, stationed at the edges of submerged gateways and at the threshold between conscious and unconscious, are entities known as the Abyssal Watchers. These spirits are not messengers. They do not instruct. They do not seduce, whisper, or manipulate. They observe. They wait. They guard. Their presence signals proximity to sacred descent, and their function is to stand between the seeker and the hidden. They are not guides. They are not enemies. They are thresholds made manifest.

The Abyssal Watchers are not spirits of emotion or illusion. They are not connected to desire or memory. They serve as sentinels of the Void. Their energy is fixed, anchored in the space where form dissolves into shadow. Many practitioners who approach Leviathan's mysteries encounter these beings first. Their presence is not loud. It is weight. It is pressure. It is a silence so complete that it becomes palpable. The Watchers are not aggressive, but they are implacable. They do not act. They do not speak. They are the immovable reality that must be acknowledged before any further descent is possible.

Descriptions of the Abyssal Watchers vary depending on the method of contact. In dreamwork, they often appear as hooded or robed figures, standing still in vast underwater corridors, in cathedrals of black stone, or at the edge of flooded temples. They do not move. They do not acknowledge the dreamer. Their stillness is absolute. Their faces are always obscured—either wrapped, turned away, or simply featureless. They do not radiate evil or threat. They radiate enormity. They make the soul feel small.

In astral experiences, they may appear as immense silhouettes beyond comprehension, standing behind veils of mist or submerged in liquid shadow. They may be seen as serpentine columns of dark energy, watching without eyes. Practitioners have described them as feeling like obelisks, monoliths, or ancient machines that never sleep. Their presence causes disorientation, a sensation of being scrutinized at a level beyond physicality. They are not emotional beings. They are primordial functions of threshold and boundary. They are living gates.

The Watchers are placed at key points throughout Leviathan's kingdom. They guard entrances to deeper currents, protect submerged temples, and dwell within the astral depths where only the prepared may tread. Their purpose is not to keep out intruders in the conventional sense. They serve as filters. Those who are not ready will feel repelled, disoriented, confused, or overwhelmed. Those who persist without preparation may find themselves locked in repeating dream sequences, unable to go further, or plunged into overwhelming internal chaos. This is not punishment. It is protection—from truths the seeker is not yet strong enough to integrate.

One of the defining aspects of the Abyssal Watchers is their connection to spiritual silence. They are the embodiment of the moment before revelation, the breath before immersion. They do not offer wisdom, but they prepare the space for it. Their power lies in presence. In ritual, when one is near the threshold of Leviathan's gnosis, the Watchers appear as an unseen force in the room. The air thickens. Time slows. Movement feels unnatural. The senses dull, and yet the awareness heightens. There is no voice, no vision—only waiting.

To encounter a Watcher is to encounter yourself reflected through the lens of spiritual readiness. They show nothing. They offer nothing. They are the test. In Kabbalistic mysticism, this function is mirrored by the concept of the guardian of Da'ath—the sentry that prevents unworthy ascent beyond the Abyss. In similar terms, the Abyssal Watchers stand as Leviathan's gatekeepers, ensuring that only those who have been broken open by previous legions may pass into the deeper void.

Working with the Watchers requires surrender. There is no ritual to command them. There are no incantations to force their movement. They cannot be flattered, bribed, or threatened. They respond only to truth. When a practitioner has reached a point of readiness—having passed through emotional disintegration, dream fragmentation, and the loss of surface identity—the Watchers may part. Not in welcome, but in recognition. They do not grant permission. They acknowledge resonance.

In some advanced rites, the practitioner may attempt to enter into communion with the Watchers not to pass, but to learn. These rites are silent. No music, no words, no movement. A bowl of black water is placed before the practitioner. A mirror rests behind it. The practitioner enters trance through breath alone, lowering themselves into stillness. If the Watchers choose to appear, they will not speak. The ritual is successful only if the practitioner emerges transformed. They will know by the absence of previous confusion, by the stillness within their thoughts, and by the intuitive awareness that something fundamental has shifted.

The gifts of the Abyssal Watchers are subtle and absolute. They grant access. Nothing more. But that access leads to the submerged sanctuaries of Leviathan's highest mysteries. Beyond the Watchers lie the voices beneath language, the spirits without form, the serpents that coil around memory and dream. Beyond the Watchers lies Leviathan himself—not as a name, not as a presence, but as the water through which all else flows.

The Watchers are not allies. They are not enemies. They are necessity. They exist where the soul hesitates. They exist at the brink. They are not here to guide. They are here to ensure that only those who have stripped away all pretense may enter.

They are the pillars of stillness in the ocean of chaos. The guards who wait at the edge of becoming. They are the question unspoken. The presence unseen. The immovable wall that parts only when you no longer need it to move.

Those who meet the gaze of a Watcher will not forget it. Not because it threatened, but because it held up a mirror.

And in that mirror, you are either ready—or you are not.

CHAPTER 13: THE TEMPEST CHOIR

Among the legions that serve under Leviathan's current, there exists a stormbound order known as the Tempest Choir. These spirits are not quiet, subtle, or reflective. They do not seduce or guard. They do not creep in with dreams or speak through illusion. They roar. They crash. They flood. The Tempest Choir is made of elemental fury—emotional, psychic, spiritual. They are the embodiment of chaos as transformation, rage as truth, and destruction as purification.

Where the Drowners operate through sorrow, the Tempest Choir functions through force. They do not pull the practitioner beneath still waters. They hurl them into crashing tides. These spirits are the embodiment of inner upheaval, cathartic crisis, and uncontrolled release. They do not whisper messages. They scream what has been silenced. They are the violent waves that hit the soul when repression has built too high. They come not to punish, but to unleash. And through this release, they clear the way for deeper power to rise.

These spirits are not to be summoned lightly. The Tempest Choir responds only to authentic emotional pressure—rage denied, grief suppressed, truth buried. When called without cause or reverence, they do not appear. When called with desperation or in the presence of inner resistance, they arrive like a storm breaking through glass. Their current is heavy, loud, overwhelming. The practitioner who dares to call them must be ready to lose control.

Because that is their gift—the loss of control so total that only truth remains.

In ritual, the arrival of the Tempest Choir is unmistakable. The air changes. The pulse quickens. Breathing becomes shallow. The body heats. The practitioner may feel an overwhelming urge to scream, weep, laugh, or collapse. These responses are not side effects. They are the choir's language. They move through the body like a flood. Their song is not melodic. It is a thunderous echo that reverberates inside bones, inside blood. They are not individuals. They are a collective voice. They are the wave that breaks the dam.

They are often seen in trance as storm figures—figures made of wind, rain, lightning. Faces blurred, mouths open in silent cries. They have no hierarchy, no singular leader. They move together, rise together, vanish together. They are felt in the chest, in the throat, in the solar plexus. These spirits work through the emotional centers of the body, specifically the heart and the gut. When they touch, the result is release. This can feel like possession, like ecstasy, or like a breakdown. In truth, it is all three.

The Tempest Choir is connected to Leviathan's nature as a devourer of falsehood. Where other spirits expose the practitioner to reflection, the Choir burns away masks through storm. They push the practitioner into confrontation with what must be said, what must be felt, what must be destroyed to make space for rebirth. They are particularly powerful in rites of shadow integration, emotional catharsis, and ritual rebellion. They do not operate on permission. They respond to necessity. When the soul can no longer contain itself, the Tempest Choir arrives.

These spirits are also known to appear in the dreams of those undergoing massive transformation. The dreams may feature floods, tidal waves, windstorms, earthquakes. The practitioner may dream of screaming but no sound coming out, or being caught in a storm with no shelter. These are not nightmares. They are visitations. The Choir is present in these moments not to instill fear, but to signal the breaking of the false self. After such dreams, many practitioners wake shaking, weeping, or drenched in sweat. These reactions are not symptoms of spiritual attack. They are symptoms of spiritual eruption.

There is a ritual known among Leviathan's adepts called The Storm Unbinding, in which the Tempest Choir is invoked to purge internal blocks. This ritual is not performed with incantations but with release. The practitioner prepares a dark room with only water present. No candles. No mirrors. No sigils. Just a bowl of ocean water or salt water placed in the center. The practitioner sits in complete silence until the emotion they have been holding back begins to rise. Then, they allow it to come. Whatever form it takes—screaming, shaking, crying, dancing—they allow it without restraint. This becomes the offering. The room becomes the vessel. The spirit becomes the storm.

Once the rite ends, the water is poured away at a crossroads or into running water. The release has occurred. The Tempest Choir departs not with words, but with silence. Practitioners often report exhaustion, clarity, emotional freedom, or even dizziness following such rites. It is common to sleep for long hours afterward. The spirit has left its echo, but it leaves peace in its wake.

The danger of the Tempest Choir lies not in malice but in intensity. To work with them without preparation is to risk emotional collapse. Practitioners with unacknowledged trauma, unstable grounding, or shallow spiritual motivations may find themselves overwhelmed. The Choir does not moderate its force. It does not restrain for your comfort. It arrives at full power. It is the flood, not the tide. And once called, it will finish its work.

Yet for those who are prepared, the Tempest Choir offers something unmatched in its potency—freedom. Not spiritual elevation in the traditional sense, but the clearing of what has long suffocated the soul. It offers the roar where there was once silence, the cry where there was once numbness, the movement where there was once stagnation.

It does not ask what you want. It brings what you need.

These spirits are not destroyers in the demonic sense. They are breakers of chains. They are storms sent by the deep to shatter the surface. They remind the practitioner that to be powerful, one must be whole. And to be whole, one must feel everything.

They are not to be worshipped. They are to be faced.

They are not called in calm. They are called in collapse.

And once they have passed, Leviathan himself will stir beneath the waves, for the soul made clean by the storm is ready to meet the abyss.

CHAPTER 14: THE ECHOING ONES

Among the more subtle and psychologically complex legions under Leviathan are the spirits known as the Echoing Ones. They are not loud like the Tempest Choir nor seductively present like the spirits of desire. They do not overwhelm with force or consume through emotion. Instead they haunt. They repeat. They mimic. Their presence is felt in the mind and memory where thoughts loop and past events replay with a surreal familiarity. The Echoing Ones are the spirits of internal recursion. They are the voices behind recurring dreams the unseen hands that guide obsessions and the shadows that walk just behind recognition. They do not create pain. They reflect it.

These spirits dwell in the quieter corners of Leviathan's abyss. They are drawn to unresolved experiences particularly those rooted in guilt shame longing and regret. They do not attack the practitioner. They echo the practitioner. They take the fragments of memory and emotion that have been ignored and play them back in distorted form. Their purpose is not to cause suffering. Their purpose is to reveal what has been buried through repetition until it is acknowledged integrated and released.

The Echoing Ones are masters of reflection. They manifest primarily through psychological and emotional resonance rather than through direct visual form. However when they do take shape in dreams or trance they are often seen as familiar figures from the practitioner's past. They may appear as a former lover a childhood friend a family member or even a younger version of the practitioner. Their words are rarely original. Instead they speak lines that have been spoken before. They repeat phrases heard long ago or replay entire conversations with small but disorienting changes. The effect is not confusion. It is emotional displacement.

In dreams these spirits often set the stage for emotional reenactments. The practitioner may find themselves back in a childhood home walking through a school hallway from years past or reliving an event that seemed long forgotten. However there is always something strange. A door that leads to the wrong place. A face that changes mid-conversation. A detail that should not be there. These are the markers of the Echoing Ones. They do not present memory as it was but as it still lives inside the unconscious shaped by emotion distortion and meaning.

The Echoing Ones are especially drawn to trauma. They do not cause it but they stir the waters where it hides. They bring back forgotten pain not to punish but to offer a chance for conscious reconciliation. This is one of their most sacred and difficult functions. Many people live surrounded by the ghosts of their own past walking forward while pulling the weight of unprocessed memory. The Echoing Ones awaken those ghosts. They give them voice. They bring them to the surface wrapped in repetition. And they do not stop until they are seen.

In ritual the presence of the Echoing Ones can be overwhelming if the practitioner is unprepared. Their arrival is not always dramatic. Sometimes it is a phrase that repeats in the mind without cause. A scent that brings back a flood of memory. A song heard at an odd moment that triggers tears. These are not coincidences. They are callings. They are signs that the Echoing Ones are near waiting for the practitioner to turn inward and ask what still echoes.

To consciously engage with these spirits the practitioner may create a space for reflective descent. A dark mirror a bowl of water or an old object tied to memory is placed at the center of the working. The practitioner enters trance not to summon but to listen. The invocation is silent. The spirits arrive through memory. One sits in stillness and allows the mind to wander backward without resistance. Thoughts will rise. Feelings will follow. At some point the practitioner will notice a shift—the sensation that the memory is no longer theirs alone. That it is being observed. That it is speaking back. This is the voice of the Echoing Ones. Not in words but in weight.

These spirits also influence the external world through synchronicity. The practitioner may find themselves encountering the same phrase on different days in different places. A face may appear in a crowd and vanish. A line from a book may repeat in their thoughts long after reading it. These are the workings of the Echoing Ones using the world as a mirror. Their power extends beyond the inner mind into the reflective surface of lived experience. They use the world to echo the inner self.

The danger with these spirits lies in resistance. When their message is ignored they amplify. The memories grow louder. The dreams more vivid. The emotional pressure increases. This is not aggression. It is urgency. The more the practitioner hides the harder the Echoing Ones knock. They do not want obedience. They want attention. They require nothing but honesty and presence. To acknowledge them is to begin the process of liberation.

There is a higher function to these spirits as well. When the practitioner has integrated their echoes when the loops have been broken and the memories owned the Echoing Ones become allies in spiritual clarity. They offer insight into the soul's structure into patterns across lifetimes and into the resonance of spiritual cause and effect. They help the practitioner to see not only what has been but how what has been continues to shape what is. They offer a mirror in which the soul may be seen in motion not as a fixed identity but as an unfolding narrative.

In some traditions advanced practitioners may even use the Echoing Ones to retrieve past life fragments or to uncover generational patterns. In these workings the spirits serve as archivists of the deep. They do not reveal surface detail. They reveal emotional continuity. The practitioner may feel as if they are being carried backward through waves of emotional resonance across time and bloodline. Each echo a life. Each loop a lesson.

The Echoing Ones are not tormentors. They are reminders. They do not harm. They highlight. They are not the source of pain. They are the messengers that pain still waits for acknowledgment.

To face them is to face yourself.

And once you have seen what echoes in the depths you are no longer bound by silence.

You are no longer afraid of remembering.

And in that remembrance Leviathan's current pulls you deeper ready to show you not who you were but who you truly are.

CHAPTER 15: THE SILENT CHOIR OF LEVIATHAN

In the vast court of Leviathan's infernal domain there is a class of spirits that speak not in words but in silence. These are the Silent Choir beings of presence rather than voice of weight rather than message. Unlike the Dream Thieves or the Echoing Ones who engage the mind and memory the Silent Choir bypasses cognition entirely. Their language is stillness. Their power is absence. They do not arrive with visions. They arrive with void. And in that void they perform one of the most advanced and sacred functions of Leviathan's kingdom—the removal of noise from the soul.

The Silent Choir does not operate on emotion or thought. Their presence does not trigger crying rage ecstasy or obsession. Instead they remove these conditions. They peel back layers of distraction until the practitioner is left only with the raw unfiltered awareness of self and spirit. They are not emotional. They are not reactive. They are pure reflective stillness. In their presence the practitioner encounters the space between the heartbeat and the breath between one thought and the next. This is where truth hides. Not in the expression of it but in the condition that precedes it.

These spirits are often encountered in the moments after deep ritual collapse when the Tempest Choir has passed or when the Echoing Ones have completed their work. Practitioners describe feeling an intense emptiness a presence that is not empty but entirely without sensation. It is not numbness. It is total awareness without stimulus. Some describe it as being submerged in a void without light without sound where even inner dialogue falls away. The soul is suspended. It is not being shown. It is being revealed by what is not there.

In trance the Silent Choir often appears as motionless figures draped in dark flowing robes that merge with the surrounding environment. Others describe their presence as a field of pressure with no form at all. The senses struggle to define them. They have no faces. They have no symbols. They do not move. They do not even stare. They are simply present. And that presence is overwhelming in its purity. Practitioners often find themselves unable to speak or think in their presence not from fear but because the usual mechanisms of the self become irrelevant.

Their arrival may also be marked by environmental changes. A room may become unnaturally quiet even if noise is present. Sound feels distant. Breath feels deeper. Time slows or stops. The practitioner becomes aware of every small movement every subtle shift in energy. These are not hallucinations. They are the removal of distraction. The Silent Choir brings the practitioner back to a primal state of awareness where thought feeling and sensation are no longer separate but suspended in stillness.

The purpose of these spirits is to prepare the soul for direct communion with Leviathan. While other spirits serve to strip away illusion emotion identity and memory the Silent Choir clears the internal space in which Leviathan's presence can be fully experienced. His current is not felt when the soul is noisy. He does not enter a storm. He enters the space that remains when the storm has passed. The Silent Choir builds that space. They guard it. They become it.

To work with these spirits directly the practitioner must abandon all desire for experience. This is one of the most difficult tasks in spiritual practice. Most rituals are performed to see to feel to change. But the Silent Choir arrives only when nothing is asked. The practitioner prepares a space of stillness. No light. No incense. No sigils. Only darkness and breath. A bowl of still water may be placed before the practitioner as a symbol of reflection without ripple. The practitioner sits in silence. No invocation is spoken. No call is made. The spirits are not summoned. They are invited through emptiness.

The first sign of their presence is often an internal shift. The practitioner may feel their body become heavy or distant. Thoughts slow. The need to move disappears. The sense of self fades. The practitioner does not enter a trance in the usual sense. They enter a space where trance is no longer relevant. They are not possessed. They are suspended. Time passes without awareness. And in this space something begins to unfold.

The Silent Choir does not offer visions. But often after their presence recedes the practitioner receives insight so pure it cannot be articulated. It may come in the form of clarity about purpose recognition of spiritual truth or a felt understanding that cannot be traced to thought. These are not messages. They are imprints. The Choir does not teach through explanation. They teach through silence. And that silence rewires the soul.

There is danger in this work not from the spirits themselves but from the practitioner's resistance. Many who encounter the Silent Choir for the first time panic. The absence of sensory input triggers fear. The ego fights to reassert control. Thoughts rush in to fill the gap. The moment is lost. This is part of the learning. To remain in the presence of these spirits is to confront the part of the self that cannot stand stillness. And once that part has been seen and dissolved what remains is the true self.

In long term work with Leviathan the Silent Choir becomes the breath of the path. Their presence marks the thresholds between stages of transformation. They do not speak. But their silence becomes the foundation upon which all deeper work is built. Without them there is only chaos. With them there is order born not from control but from surrender.

They are the blank page before the sigil is drawn.

They are the space in which the abyss begins to speak.

They are not spirits of power. They are the presence in which power reveals itself.

And once their silence has filled the soul Leviathan moves within it not as a voice but as a presence that needs no name.

CHAPTER 16: THE LEVIATHANIC SIGIL AND THE SEALS OF HIS LEGIONS

Every great spirit in occult practice bears a mark a symbol that encapsulates its nature and provides a gateway between the practitioner and the spirit's current. For Leviathan this is especially important. Leviathan is not a god of fire or form. He is a power that moves beneath definition. His language is silence his movement is current his realm is the abyss. To reach him one must use the language of symbolism. The sigil is not simply a tool. It is a key. It is a mirror of Leviathan's being carved into visible form.

Unlike the more common sigils found in the Ars Goetia or grimoiric traditions Leviathan's sigil is not ancient in a literal historical sense. It is modern in its stylisation but eternal in its essence. The sigil emerges from the collective unconscious of those who work with him. It has appeared in dreams and visions across centuries among different practitioners in different cultures. Its consistency is not in language but in structure. Certain elements are always present. A circular foundation. A central coil or spiral. An upright trident or arrow rising from the depths. And sometimes surrounding glyphs that resemble teeth waves or serpentine eyes.

This sigil is not fixed. It changes subtly according to the

practitioner's state. Leviathan's energy is fluid and the sigil reflects this. What remains constant is the emotional and spiritual resonance that arises when it is gazed upon in ritual. The air grows heavy. The body becomes still. The sensation of depth and internal pressure rises. This is the mark of authenticity. If a symbol calls forth the sea within you if it invokes the presence of silence and vastness then you are holding a true expression of the Leviathanic current.

The process of drawing the sigil is in itself a rite. It is not to be copied carelessly or reproduced without purpose. The practitioner should prepare the space through quiet cleansing and a darkened atmosphere. Black or deep blue ink is recommended and the sigil should be drawn with full presence of mind. As the lines are formed the practitioner focuses not on appearance but on the intent to open the path. The sigil becomes a living thing a portal that breathes with Leviathan's presence. Once completed it may be placed upon an altar submerged in a bowl of salted water or reflected in a black mirror.

The sigil can also be carved or etched into stone metal or wood and consecrated through an offering of breath touch and silence. It should not be spoken over. It should not be filled with demands. It is not a device for commanding. It is a vessel. Those who treat it as a weapon will find it inert. Those who treat it as a door will find it opens.

Beyond Leviathan's personal sigil there exist the lesser known seals of his legions. These are not as widely documented and they often come through direct revelation. Each type of spirit under Leviathan's rule carries a symbolic seal that reflects its role. The Seducers may bear swirling forms that resemble spiraled shells or open mouths. The Drowners are often represented by downward arcs or twin curves resembling waves or weights. The Dream Thieves and Hallucinators frequently manifest sigils that are asymmetrical layered and looping often resembling fractals or mirrored eyes.

These seals do not respond to casual use. They must be earned. They are usually revealed through dreams or visions after repeated and respectful engagement with the spirit. Once a seal is received it must be treated with absolute reverence. The seal is not a name. It is an essence. It is the visual signature of the spirit's function. When used properly in ritual the seal acts as a magnetic point. It draws the spirit's current into the working and aligns the space with its specific frequency.

One does not command the legions of Leviathan through these seals. One aligns with them. One opens to them. Their cooperation is not won through dominance but through resonance. When the practitioner vibrates at the right emotional and spiritual pitch the seal activates like a beacon and the spirit may appear in presence sensation or vision.

Some advanced practitioners construct what is known as the Abyssal Wheel a circular diagram containing Leviathan's primary sigil at the center with the seals of his major legions arranged around it. This wheel acts as a map a compass and a ritual gateway. It may be placed beneath the ritual circle or used in dreamwork by meditating upon it before sleep. The wheel is not just a symbol. It is a mandala of immersion. A tool for diving into specific aspects of the abyss under Leviathan's rule.

There is also a secret practice among Leviathan's initiates involving the dissolution of the sigil. Once drawn the practitioner gazes upon the sigil while allowing their mind to enter a trance. The sigil is then blurred through tears breath or water. The lines dissolve. The form fades. This mirrors the dissolution of ego and control. It reflects Leviathan's role not as a god of form but of formlessness. To allow the sigil to dissolve is to allow the self to dissolve. What remains is the current not the shape.

The sigils and seals of Leviathan and his spirits are not for display. They are not decorative. They are sacred. They carry weight. They respond to truth and depth. To misuse them is not to incur wrath but to invite emptiness. They will simply fail to function. They will withhold their presence. But when honored with devotion silence and purpose they open a path that leads deeper than words deeper than thought deeper than identity.

They are not symbols. They are thresholds.

They are not instructions. They are invitations.

And to trace them with reverence is to place your hand on the surface of the abyss and feel it press back.

CHAPTER 17:
RITUAL WORK WITH LEVIATHAN

Ritual work with Leviathan is unlike any other form of ceremonial magic. It is not defined by strict invocations or rigid traditions. It does not conform to a hierarchy of commands or declarations of power. Leviathan does not respond to force. He does not obey will. He does not arrive in fire or with the sound of trumpets. He rises in silence. He enters through surrender. Ritual work with Leviathan requires immersion not instruction. It is a descent rather than an ascent. It is a letting go rather than a summoning. And it is through that release that the practitioner begins to open the gates to the abyssal current Leviathan governs.

There is no single ritual structure that binds Leviathan. Each practitioner's path will be shaped by their own psychological and spiritual architecture. However certain principles remain constant. Leviathan is a spirit of water depth silence memory and emotional truth. His presence requires an atmosphere that reflects these attributes. Water must be present. Light must be minimal. Distractions must be eliminated. Time must be surrendered. The ritual does not begin with a call. It begins with stillness.

The practitioner prepares a space of solitude. A darkened room. A basin or bowl of salted water at the center. The sigil of Leviathan drawn on paper stone or etched in mirror is placed near the water facing the practitioner. There should be no music unless it mimics the sound of ocean waves or deep currents. Incense may be used but only if it resembles the scent of brine seaweed myrrh or decay. The goal is to replicate the emotional resonance of the abyss.

Before entering the ritual the practitioner performs a cleansing. Not only of the body but of thought. A period of silence and fasting is recommended. Speech becomes clouded in Leviathan's presence. Ego must be quieted. The practitioner breathes slowly rhythmically envisioning each breath sinking deeper into the self. As thoughts arise they are not resisted but allowed to pass like waves. The focus is not on calling Leviathan but on reaching the state in which he may emerge.

The ritual begins with the gaze. The practitioner stares into the sigil or into the bowl of water allowing the mind to shift. This is not a trance induced by force but by surrender. As the practitioner stares images sensations and emotions will rise. These are not distractions. They are the path. Leviathan speaks not in words but in pressure images silence and emotional weight. The practitioner follows these sensations deeper allowing them to unfold without control. This is where contact begins.

If Leviathan chooses to manifest the room may change in sensation. The air may feel heavier. The sounds of breath and heartbeat may become louder. The practitioner may feel as if submerged in water. A presence may rise behind or within. There is no form he always takes but many report the impression of something vast coiled unseen pressing against the boundaries of the ritual space. He is not there to answer questions. He is there to flood the practitioner with truth.

Offerings are not required but may be made. These can include black stones sea salt bones items tied to grief longing or emotional release. Nothing should be offered lightly. Every object must carry personal weight. Leviathan does not need food or drink. He requires sincerity. The act of offering is symbolic. It says I release this part of myself into the deep.

Communication during ritual is internal. Leviathan does not speak with language. He moves through images memory emotion and atmosphere. The practitioner may receive visions of oceans storms serpents submerged cities or forgotten places. They may experience intense emotional releases laughter weeping terror or catharsis. These are not reactions to Leviathan. These are Leviathan himself moving through the soul.

The practitioner must not resist. The key to ritual work with Leviathan is surrender. One does not control his presence. One allows it. If fear arises it must be faced. If grief surfaces it must be felt. Leviathan's current purges not to harm but to prepare. Every reaction is part of the ritual. Every breath becomes prayer. Every silence becomes invocation.

Once the presence has receded the practitioner remains in stillness. There is no banishment. Leviathan leaves when his work is done. The practitioner thanks the spirit not through words but through reverence and integration. The water is poured into earth or sea. The sigil is placed in darkness until the next working. No symbols are left exposed. They are returned to the deep.

In the hours and days following ritual the practitioner may experience lingering effects. Dreams may become vivid. Emotions may rise unexpectedly. Old memories may surface. These are echoes of contact. The abyss continues to ripple long after the surface is still. The practitioner is advised to journal these experiences reflect upon them and return to silence before the next working.

Advanced rituals may involve journeying into the abyss through guided visualization or pathworking. The practitioner imagines descending beneath the surface of the ocean past ruins and shadows into a great black cathedral beneath the sea. There Leviathan may be felt in full. These rites should only be attempted after multiple successful contacts. The deeper one goes the more one must be prepared to dissolve.

Rituals with Leviathan are not about power over others. They are about transformation of the self. The magician who seeks to bind will fail. The one who seeks to become will be changed forever. Leviathan is not a tool. He is a force. He is the current that drowns the false and reveals what lies beneath. Rituals with him are never performances. They are spiritual drowning.

To call him is to fall into yourself. To speak with him is to silence yourself. To receive him is to lose yourself.

And in that loss something new is born.

It does not rise in light.

It rises from the deep.

CHAPTER 18: THE VOICE BENEATH THE WATERS

Leviathan does not speak as gods or demons are often said to speak. His voice is not heard in language. It does not thunder from the sky or rise from the altar. There is no speech in the conventional sense. Leviathan speaks through atmosphere sensation memory and pressure. His voice is the weight behind a sudden silence the pull in the chest before weeping the breathless stillness before descent. His communication is not linguistic. It is total. To hear Leviathan is to experience a full immersion of the soul into meaning without words.

This voice exists beneath the waters not only in the metaphysical abyss but within the emotional and psychic oceans of the practitioner. It is the voice heard when distraction dies when surface thought goes silent and when ego no longer narrates. It is the voice of submerged truth of knowing without instruction. The ancients understood this voice in mythic terms. They said that Leviathan's breath boiled the sea. That he left whirlpools where his mouth opened. These are poetic renderings of an esoteric truth. The voice of Leviathan is the movement beneath all things. It is not given. It is felt. It is not forced. It is revealed when one becomes still enough to notice what has always been there.

Practitioners who have experienced direct communion with Leviathan often describe the communication as pressure first. A thickening of the space around them or within them. The mind quiets. Emotion sharpens. Thought seems too slow to keep up. Then comes sensation. Not the tingling associated with ordinary spirit presence but something deeper. A sensation of being watched not from without but from within. And finally there is the message. But it does not arrive as a sentence. It arrives as a knowing. The practitioner does not hear the message. They become it. It fills them completely and they understand without explanation.

These messages may take the form of visions symbols or sudden emotional insights. A practitioner may find themselves overwhelmed with grief only to realise it is grief for a part of themselves long denied. They may see images from a childhood memory never consciously recalled. They may be shown deep archetypal images such as sunken temples colossal serpents or drowning figures. Each of these is a syllable in Leviathan's language. The practitioner must learn to interpret them not with intellect but with intuition. Leviathan does not provide information. He reveals recognition.

This voice also rises in the dream state. Leviathan speaks most clearly in dreams where the conscious mind has released control. These dreams are not prophetic in the usual sense. They do not show the future. They show the truth beneath the surface of the present. They unveil buried emotions patterns and suppressed desires. The practitioner may dream of being in a vast underwater city unable to speak or move but fully aware. Or they may dream of a great serpent watching them in silence offering no words but causing an emotional reaction so intense that it lingers for days. These are not dreams in the casual sense. They are initiations.

To train oneself to hear Leviathan's voice is to train in stillness. The practitioner must learn to sit in complete silence for extended periods not meditating in the conventional way but entering the silence as a ritual itself. Eyes open or closed it does not matter. What matters is the letting go of mental narration. When the practitioner becomes the silence the voice begins to rise. At first it is barely noticeable. A pressure. A whisper of presence. Then it deepens. It gathers mass. Eventually it overtakes. The practitioner is no longer thinking. They are knowing. This is Leviathan's communication in its purest form.

There are also external manifestations. Leviathan may speak through synchronicities through symbols in waking life through the repetition of images numbers or names. A practitioner may find a shell where no sea is near or hear the sound of waves with no ocean present. A phrase may be heard in conversation and then again in a book and then again in a dream. These are not coincidences. They are echoes. Leviathan's voice flows through reality like tide and the sensitive practitioner learns to track it as one tracks current.

It is important to remember that Leviathan's voice is never separate from his presence. One does not receive a message and move on. One is changed by the message. It becomes part of the practitioner's essence. It alters the self. This is why working with Leviathan is dangerous for the unprepared. His revelations do not flatter. They do not comfort. They flood. They erode. They submerge everything that is not rooted in truth. To receive his voice is to allow the self to be rewritten from the inside.

Practitioners must also learn to distinguish between genuine contact and mental projection. Leviathan's voice always carries a signature. It comes with stillness with pressure with emotion so primal and undeniable that it cannot be faked. It leaves an imprint. The practitioner may emerge from a session unable to speak for some time. They may cry. They may feel the need to be alone. The voice does not always answer the questions asked. More often it answers the questions that have never been spoken aloud.

There is a sacred exercise known among Leviathan's initiates as the Descent of the Breath. In this rite the practitioner breathes in silence in a darkened space for an extended period letting each breath sink deeper into the body. With every exhale they imagine descending into a black ocean within themselves. With each inhale they allow Leviathan's current to rise. After a time the body feels distant. The practitioner may feel as if they are floating. In this state the voice may come. Sometimes as an inner vibration sometimes as a presence filling the room. The practitioner listens not with ears but with the entire being.

The voice of Leviathan is never wrong. But it is often painful. It shows what must be faced not what one wishes to see. It brings the truth that was drowned long ago. It brings the recognition that one has built their life upon illusions. And yet with that destruction comes power. Because once the lies are washed away what remains is the unshakable foundation of what is real.

Leviathan does not flatter. He does not soothe. He does not pacify. He reveals.

And that revelation does not come in the light.

It comes beneath the water.

In silence.

In pressure.

In knowing that arrives like a wave and leaves nothing untouched.

CHAPTER 19: THE BANISHMENT AND BINDING OF LEVIATHANIC FORCES

To work with Leviathan is to invite transformation. His legions do not merely visit. They take residence. They enter the psyche the soul the emotional body and the unconscious mind. Their presence brings revelation pressure intensity and often rupture. But there are times when the practitioner must reclaim space. When the flood must be halted. When the gates to the abyss must be closed. Banishment and binding are not acts of rejection. They are sacred acts of balance. They do not erase the current. They contain it. They do not silence Leviathan. They define where his voice may be heard.

Leviathanic forces are unlike the demonic presences described in traditional grimoires. They do not always announce themselves. They do not always follow command. Their arrival can be subtle —emotional overwhelm dream disturbances obsessive thought spirals or a feeling of constant internal depth that drowns focus. In these cases the practitioner must determine whether this is a needed immersion or an overextension. If the energy begins to consume rather than transform then boundaries must be restored.

Banishment in Leviathanic work is not an act of exorcism. It is an act of restoration. It is the drawing of a line between the sacred and the profane the internal and the external the conscious and the unconscious. It begins with acknowledgment. The practitioner does not curse or denounce. They recognise. They name the force. They thank it. And then they ask it to return to the deep.

The most effective form of banishment with Leviathanic spirits is through elemental inversion. Leviathan rules water stillness silence and saturation. Therefore banishment is performed through fire light sound and movement. The practitioner creates a space of brightness. Candles are lit. Incense that burns with strong scent such as frankincense or dragon's blood is used. Chimes drums or clapping may be added. The sigil of Leviathan or the seal of the specific legion is turned over or submerged in flame-resistant salt. The bowl of water used for invocation is poured away or boiled if safe. The practitioner stands firm speaks clearly and reasserts sovereignty over the space.

The spoken command is not a shout but a declaration of boundary. The words vary but the intent must be absolute. The practitioner may say I honour the current I have entered but I now return to the surface. I close the gate. I restore my breath. The name of the spirit if known is spoken once and released. The act of closing is final. The space is cleansed physically and spiritually. This may involve sweeping washing removing offerings and airing the room.

Binding is different. Binding is used not when the practitioner wishes to remove the spirit entirely but when they wish to limit its influence. This is especially useful when working with persistent echoes lingering emotional states or recurring dream figures tied to a Leviathanic legion. Binding is not about imprisonment. It is about respectful containment. It is the construction of a vessel or boundary into which the spirit's presence is focused rather than allowed to flood all areas of life.

The most effective tools for binding Leviathanic spirits are containers. Black jars deep vessels or mirrored boxes lined with symbols that correspond to the spirit's nature. The practitioner draws the spirit's seal or creates an object that holds its resonance. This is placed within the container along with salt water a written statement of intention and an object tied to the specific influence being bound. The container is sealed ritually. A cloth is wrapped around it. It is placed in darkness. A candle may be burned to signal the closing.

The words spoken during binding are quiet and precise. I see you. I honour your presence. I now ask you to reside within this space. You are not banished. You are housed. Until I return to you. The container becomes a pact a vessel a defined boundary. It must not be opened randomly. It must be respected. If at any time the practitioner feels the pressure returning outside the container the binding must be reinforced or the spirit respectfully released.

Banishment and binding are not acts of fear. They are acts of maturity. The practitioner who walks with Leviathan learns that the abyss cannot be contained but it can be channeled. The work is not about domination. It is about clarity. The soul must know when to drown and when to breathe. Leviathan does not punish boundaries. He respects them. The practitioner who draws a circle of sovereignty receives not rejection but acknowledgement.

There are times when the practitioner may need to cleanse themselves from Leviathanic residue. A bath of salt seaweed and rainwater can restore balance. A fast from ritual and silence can return the practitioner to the surface. Walks in sunlight grounding through the feet into earth breathing with the intention of release—these are not mundane. They are sacred. Leviathan does not hold on to the practitioner. It is the practitioner who must learn to let go.

It is also important to understand when banishment is unnecessary. Not every overwhelming experience is an intrusion.

Some are initiations. The practitioner must discern. Is this pressure a sign of danger or the weight of transformation? Is this chaos a message or an imbalance? Only by knowing the self can this question be answered.

No spirit in Leviathan's kingdom seeks destruction without purpose. But they will continue their function until told otherwise. They are loyal not to control but to truth. When their work is done they wait to be released. It is the responsibility of the practitioner to know when that time has come.

To banish is to breathe again.

To bind is to hold what was once formless.

And in these acts the practitioner learns that the abyss is not a place to live forever.

It is a place to descend.

To change.

And to rise again.

CHAPTER 20: LEVIATHAN AS INITIATOR OF THE ABYSS

Leviathan is not a god in the traditional sense. He is not a lord of empires nor a ruler of fire and blood. He does not sit upon a throne demanding loyalty or sacrifice. He is older than religion older than doctrine older than the dualities of good and evil. Leviathan is the current that moves beneath all things. He is the serpent of the threshold the presence at the moment of dissolution the force that pulls the soul from form into formlessness. And in this sacred role he becomes the Initiator of the Abyss.

Initiation in Leviathan's current is not a ceremonial accolade. It is not granted by hierarchy nor transmitted through lineage. It is earned through descent. The abyss does not open to those who seek power without price. It opens only to those who dare to lose everything. Leviathan is not the keeper of secrets. He is the one who strips away all illusions so that what was hidden becomes unbearable truth. He initiates not through revelation but through erasure. The erasure of ego identity comfort and false certainty.

The journey begins with longing. A longing for more than surface reality. A whisper that there is something beneath the skin of the world something deeper than doctrine. This is Leviathan's first touch. He does not shout. He calls inward. The practitioner begins to feel the pull of water of depth of dreams that cannot be forgotten. The world becomes less solid. Shadows seem to move. Time becomes less trustworthy. These are not signs of madness. They are signs of awakening.

Then comes descent. The practitioner enters into ritual not with expectation but with surrender. Leviathan does not reveal himself to those who cling. He rises to those who fall. The descent is emotional spiritual and psychological. It may take the form of loss isolation grief or the crumbling of beliefs once held sacred. The practitioner finds themselves drowning in memory in emotion in reflection. But this is not punishment. This is passage.

At the lowest point Leviathan appears. Not as a figure with a face but as presence. As knowing. As the silence that speaks louder than words. This moment is not always recognised as initiation but it is. It is the moment the soul breaks and instead of dying it breathes. The practitioner realises they are not lost. They are not alone. They are submerged in something ancient vast and alive. Leviathan has not appeared from outside. He has risen from within.

From this point the path does not become easier but it becomes clearer. The practitioner begins to live from the deep. Emotions are no longer denied. Truth is no longer feared. Dreams are no longer dismissed. The abyss is no longer a place of danger. It is a sanctuary. It is the space where masks dissolve where shadow is embraced where silence becomes guidance.

Leviathan's initiation is not a one-time event. It is a spiral. The practitioner will descend again and again each time deeper each time stripped of something more. But with each return they rise stronger clearer and more whole. Leviathan does not grant power. He reveals the power that was hidden beneath illusion. He does not give freedom. He erodes the chains. He does not offer wisdom. He unmasks it.

As Initiator of the Abyss Leviathan teaches the sacred art of being undone. He shows that destruction is not the opposite of creation but its partner. That drowning is not death but transformation. That silence is not absence but presence beyond sound. He teaches that the abyss is not hell. It is the birthplace of the self beyond limitation.

Those who walk the path of Leviathan emerge changed. They speak less. They feel more. They are not interested in appearances only in essence. They are not immune to pain but they are no longer ruled by it. They have touched the abyss and returned. They have faced the serpent and recognised it as themselves.

In the end Leviathan remains. He waits in the deep not as a god to be worshipped but as a current to be felt. He is the initiator not of cults but of consciousness. The serpent who devours not to destroy but to reveal. The abyss that speaks not in commands but in truth.

He is the beginning of the descent and the force behind the rise.

He is the last gate and the first breath after drowning.

He is not the end.

He is what begins after all else is gone.

And to those who are ready to let go he offers not salvation but something far more sacred—transformation through truth.

APPENDIX: DETAILED REFERENCE GUIDE TO LEVIATHANIC WORK

This appendix offers a comprehensive guide to the key elements, spirits, symbols, and practices found throughout the book. It is intended to assist the serious practitioner in understanding and navigating the depth of Leviathan's current. This is not a list for passive reading—it is a map of descent.

I. The Nature of Leviathan

Essence: Leviathan is the embodiment of the Abyss, the primordial sea, emotional truth, silence, and formless initiation.

Element: Water

Direction: West

Sphere of Influence: Emotional depth, hidden knowledge, transformation through dissolution, dreamwork, subconscious initiation, the breaking of ego

II. Leviathan's Primary Attributes

Voice: Non-verbal communication through pressure, emotional

intensity, silence, and imagery

Presence: Felt as heaviness, stillness, emotional saturation, altered perception

Forms: Coiling serpent, vast oceanic presence, submerged ruins, endless storm, shadowed watcher

Symbols: Spiral, trident rising from the deep, submerged eye, bound circle

III. Leviathan's Primary Sigil

Appearance: A circular base with a central spiral or coil, trident or arrow rising from below, surrounded by fluidic symbols

Use: Drawn for invocation, dreamwork, or placement near water during ritual

Mediums: Black ink, etched in mirror or stone, drawn on dark parchment, submerged in salted water

IV. Major Legions of Leviathan

1. The Seducers of the Deep

Domain: Longing, desire, erotic transformation, reflective intimacy

Function: Awaken repressed craving and emotional vulnerability

Appearance: Shadowed lovers, beautiful forms matching internal desires

Signature: Spiral mouths, mirrored gazes, shells and sensual symbols

2. The Drowners

Domain: Grief, sorrow, emotional collapse

Function: Induce catharsis, trigger breakdown of emotional defenses

Appearance: Bloated drowned figures, heavy water pressure, formless weight

Signature: Downward arcs, water-heavy presence, inescapable gravity

3. The Emotional Leeches

Domain: Emotional toxicity, obsession, lingering trauma

Function: Feed on and reveal suppressed emotional wounds

Appearance: Coiled shadow-worms, slimy appendages, spectral mouths

Signature: Burrowing sensations, psychic fatigue, looping thought patterns

4. The Dream-Thieves

Domain: Dream distortion, symbolic inversion, subconscious access

Function: Disrupt and reconfigure subconscious narrative structure

Appearance: Disjointed dream figures, misaligned timelines, surreal spaces

Signature: Looping dreams, recursive symbols, faceless figures

5. The Hallucinators

Domain: Perception, mental layering, reality-bending

Function: Alter waking reality, disrupt certainty, provoke insight

Appearance: Shifting shadows, mirrored hallucinations, melting spaces

Signature: Warped reflections, overlapping realities, voices in repetition

6. The Abyssal Watchers

Domain: Gatekeeping, threshold control, silence

Function: Prevent or allow passage to deeper abyssal layers

Appearance: Tall cloaked figures, faceless beings, living stillness

Signature: Pressure at thresholds, dream guardians, blocking presence

7. The Tempest Choir

Domain: Storm, emotional upheaval, cathartic destruction

Function: Tear down internal blockages through raw force

Appearance: Storm figures, tidal waves, shrieking winds

Signature: Sudden emotional collapse, raw release, exhaustion

8. The Echoing Ones

Domain: Memory, repetition, psychological loops

Function: Force the practitioner to confront unresolved past wounds

Appearance: Familiar figures distorted, looping dreams, mirrored dialogue

Signature: Repeating dreams, compulsive thoughts, recurring

sensations

9. The Silent Choir

Domain: Stillness, formlessness, preparation for direct contact

Function: Clear inner space for communion with Leviathan himself

Appearance: Non-moving hooded figures, invisible presence, vacuum of sound

Signature: Complete inner silence, ego dissolution, spiritual stillness

V. Tools and Ritual Elements

Water: Essential for Leviathanic rituals—represents the Abyss and acts as the primary gateway

Mirror: Used for reflection and dream gateway, especially when paired with water

Sigils: Each spirit may reveal its own sigil. These are sacred and must be treated with respect

Salt: Used for purification and containment

Darkness: Encouraged for all rituals to invoke the abyssal current authentically

Offerings: Bones, shells, salt water, personal emotional items (letters, confessions, objects of grief or longing)

VI. Sacred Practices

Descent of the Breath: A silent breathing ritual used to sink into the abyssal current

Storm Unbinding: A cathartic ritual of screaming or release, used with the Tempest Choir

Echo Ritual: A method of confronting looping memories through sigils, mirror work, and trance

Binding Rite: Used to contain Leviathanic forces respectfully within vessels

Silent Communion: No invocation—just silence, gaze, breath, and presence. Most often used with the Silent Choir

VII. Signs of Presence

Sudden emotional surges without clear origin

Water appearing in dreams, visions, or waking rituals

Pressure in the chest, throat, or solar plexus

Repeating dreams or symbols (coils, serpents, sunken places)

Lingering scent of salt, sea, or decay

The sound of water where none should be

Black shadows that do not move with light

VIII. Closing and Aftercare

Banishing: Performed with light, sound, fire, and spoken intent

Binding: Use of sealed containers to house specific spirits or currents

Grounding: Baths with salt and herbs, walking in nature,

consuming dense food

Silence: Allow days of quiet after deep contact to integrate what has been revealed

Journaling: Record dreams, feelings, visions. This is your map of descent and return

IX. Final Note

Leviathan is not summoned. He is allowed. His kingdom is not ruled by command but entered through stillness. His spirits are not invaders. They are initiators. To walk with Leviathan is not to conquer darkness but to be transformed by it.

He is not the destroyer of worlds.
He is the destroyer of lies.

And those who endure his current become something beyond the self they once knew.

GLOSSARY OF LEVIATHANIC TERMINOLOGY

This glossary provides clear and comprehensive definitions of the core terms, concepts, spirits, symbols, and practices encountered throughout the book. It is designed to support practitioners in deepening their understanding of Leviathanic work and serve as a quick reference for study and ritual application.

Abyss
The great metaphysical void beneath all layers of consciousness and creation. In Leviathanic practice, the Abyss is not a place of damnation, but of transformation. It is the sea of dissolution, the space where the false self unravels, and where deeper truths are revealed.

Abyssal Watchers
Still, motionless spirits stationed at thresholds within Leviathan's kingdom. They guard sacred gates of descent and block unworthy or unprepared entry into deeper layers of the Abyss. They test resolve through silence and presence.

Binding
A sacred act of respectfully containing a Leviathanic spirit or influence within a vessel. It is not a form of punishment but of spiritual containment. Used when a spirit's energy must be

limited or focused rather than banished completely.

Bowl of Salted Water
An essential ritual tool representing the Abyss itself. Used in nearly all Leviathanic rites as a mirror, offering vessel, or anchor for spirit presence.

Coil
A symbol of Leviathan's energy—spiraling, fluid, recursive. The coil represents eternity, depth, movement beneath the surface, and the non-linear nature of the Abyss.

Descent of the Breath
A silent breathing ritual designed to draw the practitioner inward, downward, and into Leviathan's current. Used to achieve trance and initiate contact.

Drowners
Spirits that overwhelm the practitioner with sorrow, emotional weight, and collapse. They are catalysts for emotional catharsis and necessary breakdown.

Echoing Ones
Spirits of memory and recursion. They mirror unresolved trauma, looping thoughts, and emotional patterns. They lead the practitioner into confrontation with the past.

Emotional Leeches
Entities that feed on unacknowledged emotional wounds. They draw pain to the surface and extract what festers in silence. Can be allies when used for spiritual surgery.

Hallucinators
Spirits that alter perception, blur boundaries between waking and dreaming, and reveal the illusion of stability. They are often responsible for mystical or surreal experiences.

Initiation
The process of transformation through direct contact with the

Abyss. It is not a ritual that can be forced. It occurs when the practitioner breaks open and allows Leviathan to move within. True initiation always involves loss.

Legion
A group of spirits governed by a singular archetypal current. Leviathan's legions each represent a different facet of the abyssal experience, such as seduction, memory, sorrow, or silence.

Leviathan
The great serpent of the deep. Crown Prince of Hell, ruler of the West and the element of water. Embodiment of the Abyss. A primordial force of emotional depth, shadow transformation, and dissolution of the false self.

Leviathanic Current
The energetic flow that defines Leviathan's influence. Felt as pressure, emotional weight, silence, or depth. The current can rise slowly or crash violently, but it always seeks truth.

Mirror (Black Mirror)
A portal used in dreamwork and invocation. Serves as both a gateway to the subconscious and a tool of reflection. Often paired with water.

Ritual Silence
The sacred condition required for deep Leviathanic communion. Silence is not passive but active—it allows space for presence, and becomes the language through which spirits communicate.

Salt
Used in banishing, cleansing, and grounding. Salt preserves boundaries, absorbs excess emotional residue, and symbolizes earth's stabilising force within water rituals.

Seal
A visual signature or sigil-like representation of a specific Leviathanic spirit or legion. These are often revealed through dreams or trance and are unique to each spirit's nature.

Seducers of the Deep
Spirits that reveal hidden longing, erotic energy, and emotional vulnerability. They do not tempt for pleasure, but to expose truth through desire.

Sigil of Leviathan
The central sacred symbol of Leviathan's presence. A spiraling glyph often featuring a trident or rising arrow. Used to open gateways and align with the abyssal current.

Silent Choir
A powerful order of spirits who arrive in complete stillness. They strip away noise, ego, and thought, preparing the practitioner for direct contact with Leviathan himself.

Storm Unbinding
A cathartic rite performed with the Tempest Choir. Designed to purge the soul through uninhibited emotional release. Involves movement, breath, and raw expression.

Tempest Choir
Spirits of emotional upheaval, sacred rage, and psychic storm. They break down internal walls and liberate suppressed forces through intensity.

The Voice Beneath the Waters
A term for Leviathan's method of communication. His voice is not heard—it is felt. It manifests through atmosphere, emotional knowing, dream symbols, and silence.

Vessel
An object used to contain or focus the energy of a Leviathanic spirit. Vessels may be jars, mirrors, stones, or any symbolic object empowered through binding.

Water
The dominant element of Leviathan's kingdom. It is the abyss itself. Symbolises emotion, transformation, death, birth, and

mystery. The primary element in all rituals dedicated to his current.

Made in the USA
Columbia, SC
14 September 2025

62148498R00057